# Conquering Fear

# *Conquering Fear*

*A thirty-one-day guide to overcoming fear*

## *By*
## *Dr. Roger L. Frye*

LATTE **Brothers**
COMMUNICATIONS

Conquering Fear
Original Copyright © 2006 by Roger L. Frye
Revised Second Edition Copyright © 2011

Published by:
Latte Brothers Communications Press
1030 E. Hwy 377 Suite 110 Box 184
Granbury, TX 76048
www.LatteBros.com

Request for information should be addressed to:
Leland Publications, 1208 Clearwood Ct., Allen, TX 75002

Cover Design by Barry Jenkins

ISBN-978-0-9834869-1-6

Printed in the United States of America.

# ENDORSEMENTS

Wow! This is one of the most captivating books I have ever read. Roger Frye is a gifted teacher with the God-given ability to make things clear. He communicates truth with great hope and faith. It makes the process of discovery and getting free from fear an anticipation of joy. This book is a must for any person serious about growing up in Christ."

**Olen Griffing**
*Founder, Antioch Oasis International Network*

*Conquering Fear* is a book that is both practical and relevant for today. Many people suffer from various forms of fear that keep them from accomplishing and becoming the Champions God has called them to be. There are over 3000 known fears we must overcome. Roger Frye has developed a daily devotion that enables you to face fear and put fear under your feet. As you walk through the pages of this book your spirit will become stronger.

**Barbie Breathitt**
*Breath of the Spirit Ministries, Inc.*

If you are reading this, don't put the book down. Roger Frye, a friend, a pastor, and a man after God's heart, has heard the cries of many people through his multifaceted ministry of over 3 decades. The cries for help are often locked up by fear in dark hidden places created by experiences, people, and our choices. This book provides the keys to unlock the crippling pain of fear-driven lives. Each day the Holy Spirit seems to speak to the needs of the reader as only He can. Roger relates personal stories and events in his own life, draws on the experiences of those he has counseled, and underscores everything with the Word of God as he offers solutions and prayers.

**Rev. John T. Clifford**
*Founding Pastor, Faith Church of Collin County, Texas*

Roger Frye has made it easy for all of us to identify areas of fear and how to break free. I found his biblical application to be enlightening and challenging. This book is a needed tool in today's families who want to live in God's fullness.

**Kerry Kirkwood**
*Senior Pastor, Trinity Fellowship, Tyler, Texas*

I have never seen another book like it on the subject. Roger Frye has done an outstanding job of revealing the numerous faces of fear.

**Henry Malone**
*President, Vision Life Ministries*

*I dedicate this book to my wife Ruthie, who has stood with me through thick and thin for over 40 years. She has been my faithful best friend and without her help I would not be the man I am today. God continues to bless me with her wisdom and her unwavering commitment to the Lord.*

# Disclaimer

*Conquering Fear* does not seek to be in conflict with any medical or psychiatric practices. The information here is intended for your spiritual growth and general knowledge. It is not intended to be a substitute for medical or psychiatric advice or treatment for specific medical or psychological conditions or disorders.

# Foreward

Fear is an emotion with which all of us are acquainted. Fear is no stranger to the believer as well as the unbeliever. 2 Timothy 1:7, NKJV, *"For God has not given us a spirit of fear, but of power and of love and of a sound mind."* Although we know that God is not the author of fear, we seem to keep on struggling with the many facets of fear.

Roger Frye has done an outstanding job of revealing the numerous faces of fear. Though much has been previously written on this subject, I believe this is a "must read book." Pastor Frye presents fear from viewpoints that few others have expounded upon. Each chapter is a short snapshot that focuses on a different facet of fear. Conquering Fear will hold your attention as you read it and realize how fear has deeply affected your life.

The tragedy in the Body of Christ is that too many do not seem to understand that we do not have to keep living under the power and influence of fear. Yes, we all face fear, but we do not have to be controlled by it. Jesus never intended for us to be captured and controlled by any form of fear. Pastor Frye does an excellent job of showing how to defeat fear in your life. He challenges us all to rise above what Satan is doing and live in all that Jesus has died to give us. He makes us want to be an overcomer, not be overcome. He challenges us to be a victor, not a victim. Read and receive revelation and insight to make fear your slave.

**Henry Malone, President**
*Vision Life Ministries*

# Contents

# Acknowledgments

*I wish to express my deepest gratitude to Francisca Kennedy-Ellis for her work in editing the rough draft of this book on fear. I thank her for her supportive role in completing the book.*

*I want to say thank you to my dear friends, Bill and Ceil Hoffman, who encouraged me to write a book several years ago.*

*I am grateful for the team members at a Barbie Breathitt "Destiny Calls" seminar who encouraged me to write. Their words motivated me to take up again the task of writing, which I had put on the back burner for quite some time.*

*I want to thank Elizabeth (Marshall) Hunter for her assistance in editing and proofreading the final draft. I am also deeply appreciative of my other friends who offered insightful comments.*

*I want to acknowledge the special friends and partners who contributed financially to underwrite the publication of "Conquering Fear." Thank you for being willing to invest in the lives of people who will be benefited by reading this book.*

*And finally, special thanksgiving goes to my Pastor, John Clifford, and the dear members of Faith Church. Their unwavering support has significantly impacted my life.*

# Introduction

This book does not seek to approach the subject of fear from the perspective of psychology but instead looks at this troubling emotion through the eyes of a pastor. It deals with fear on a spiritual rather than psychological level. It flows from the vantage point of a pastor's heart that yearns for God's people to experience greater levels of freedom. It is meant to be devotional in nature, not a psychological treatise or technical work.

The book is divided into short chapters that deal with various forms of fear. It is designed for you to go through a chapter a day for 31 days as part of your daily quiet time with God. Each chapter begins with a related scripture and ends with a prayer.

As a part of the prayers, you are instructed to actually speak to the fear as though it were an entity. This may be a little uncomfortable for some readers but there truly is a Biblical basis for this approach.

One Sabbath day Jesus taught in a synagogue and afterwards went to the home of Simon Peter to eat dinner. But Peter's mother-in-law was sick with a fever so they asked Jesus to heal her. *Now He arose from the synagogue, and entered Simon's house. But Simon's wife's mother was sick with a high fever, and they made request of Him concerning her. So He stood over her and rebuked the fever, and it left her. And immediately she arose and served them* (Luke 4:38-39). It is interesting how Jesus responded. He did not stop and pray that the Father would heal her and take the fever away. Instead He rebuked the fever and it left her. In other words, He spoke to the fever. He addressed the illness.

The word "rebuked" in the Greek is *epitimao*. It means to reprove, chide, censure, rebuke, reprimand, and admonish strongly. It is the same word used in reference to His confrontation with a demon earlier that day in the synagogue. *But Jesus rebuked him, saying, "Be quiet, and come out of him!" And when the demon had thrown him in their midst, it came out of him, and did not hurt him* (Luke 4:35). Just as Jesus spoke to and rebuked the demon, in like manner He spoke to the fever in Peter's mother-in-law.

When I first saw this truth from scripture I thought I would put it into practice on my wife Ruthie. She had been plagued with cold sores for many years of our marriage. She would get big ugly blisters on her lip that would scab over and make her feel self-conscious. The cold sores would recur about every three to six weeks and always last a full week. After several years of suffering we finally discovered an amino acid supplement that cut down the frequency and duration to a degree but the problem still persisted.

One evening she got a fresh outbreak on her lip so I asked her if I could pray for her in a new way. I said something like this, "You cold sore, I rebuke you in the name of Jesus. I command you to leave her lip and don't return. Jesus defeated you at the cross so leave her now!" To our delight, when she woke up the next morning the cold sore was completely gone.

No cold sores appeared for about a year. Then one Sunday morning before church we noticed a big bump on her lip—the precursor to a cold sore. I said, "I don't know why it came back but let me deal with it the same way I did last time." So I rebuked it authoritatively and within ten minutes it was completely gone! Dealing with disease in this manner was definitely out of my comfort zone but I was thrilled with the results. Since then I have witnessed numerous maladies disappear instantaneously by simply rebuking them sternly.

Jesus taught us to speak to our mountain. A mountain is an obstacle or problem in our life. Jesus said, *"For assuredly, I say to you, whoever says to this mountain, 'Be removed and be cast into the sea,' and does not doubt in his heart, but believes that those things he says will be done, he will have whatever he says"* (Mark 11:23). Don't talk only to God about your mountain—learn to talk to your mountain about God.[i]

Jesus goes on to say, *"Therefore I say to you, whatever things you ask when you pray, believe that you receive them, and you will have them"* (Mark 11:24). What Jesus is saying is that there is another way to pray. You can pray to God about your mountain or you can speak to your mountain about your God. Fear can be a huge mountain in your life. Learn to speak to the fears in your life about how Jesus defeated them and command them to leave.

This practice may be extremely uncomfortable for you at first but I encourage you to step out of your comfort zone. Boldly speak to your mountain and command it to go. Jesus gave you this authority so use it.

Can individuals rid themselves of fear? Yes and no. Although much work can be accomplished independently, we usually need a trained, Spirit-filled Christian to help us gain higher degrees of freedom. For instance, a back surgeon would never think of performing surgery on himself. Likewise, we need each other's help to heal our emotional wounds. God devised the body of Christ to be interdependent—not independent. We need each other's help in becoming all God wants us to be.

My prayer is that God will use this book to help you identify specific fears that may be at work in your life. Recognition is the starting place. Once you recognize them I also want to give you some tools to help dismantle the stronghold of fear. Personally, I have a whole lot less fear than I used to have, and oh, what a blessing it is. May the grace of God be upon your life as you do your part in becoming free.

# 1

## Freedom From Fear

*For God has not given us a spirit of fear, but of power and of love and of a sound mind.*

*(2 Timothy 1:7)*

S everal years ago I attended a seminar where they were teaching on the subject of the spiritual roots of disease. At the break I approached the leader and asked, "Do you suppose there is a spiritual root behind my chronic back pain?" He looked in my eyes and said one word, "Fear." Out of politeness I smiled and thanked him but as I walked away I said indignantly to myself, "He's mistaken on this one. I don't have any fear in my life." Later I thought, "If there is fear in my life it won't hurt to ask God to show me."

Thank God, I had sense enough to say to the Lord, "God, I don't see it, but if it's true I have fear in my life, reveal it to me." (By the way, one of the most rewarding things you can pray is, "God, help me to see me as You see me." I challenge you to try it and listen to what the Holy Spirit tells you.) When I did, the Holy Spirit began to shine His spotlight on various forms of fear present in me. Astonishingly, when I dealt with it, the back pain went away. Glory to God – I am free from chronic back pain as well as other physical problems including acute acid reflux. I tell you this story to help you see that fear often remains hidden.

God answered that prayer and, to my amazement, many forms of fear began to surface and come to the light. So I began to deal with these fears one at a time. After awhile, to my delight, I began to experience a new level of victory in my Christian walk. I began to understand that in the past the way I dealt with fear was to pretend it wasn't there. God didn't give me the fear and God didn't want it in my life.

In the above key verse the New International Version of the Bible translates the word *fear* as *timidity*.[ii] Notice, however, that the root word in the Greek is *deilos* and can be translated as *fearful, timidity, afraid, and cowardice,* all of which are forms of fear. The same word is found in Mark 4:37-40 where we find the story of the disciples when they were caught in a violent storm in the midst of the sea and they feared for their lives. *And a great windstorm arose, and the waves beat into the boat, so that it was already filling. But He was in the stern, asleep on a pillow. And they awoke Him, and said to Him, "Teacher, do You not care that we are perishing?" Then He arose and rebuked the wind, and said to the sea, "Peace, be still!" And the wind ceased and there was a great calm. But He said to them, "Why are you so fearful (deilos)? How is it that you have no faith?"* The word timidity in the New International Version of 2 Timothy 1:7 conveys the idea of shyness or lack of self-confidence, but it is obvious from the response of the disciples that the word deilos can be far more intense than that connotation.

Keep in mind that there exists such a thing as good fear. For example, scripture repeatedly exhorts us to fear the LORD, and if we do, blessings will follow. In Proverbs 22:4 we are encouraged to fear the LORD. *By humility and the fear of the LORD are riches, and honor, and life.* Again in Proverbs 1:7 it states, *The fear of the LORD is the beginning of knowledge: but fools despise wisdom and instruction. The fear of the LORD prolongs days, but the years of the wicked shall be shortened* (Proverbs 10:27). Great blessings come to those who fear the LORD. However, people often misunderstand the fear of the LORD. Let me emphasize that it is not the kind of fear that makes us cower away from God in fright. To the contrary, it is a holy respect and reverential awe that attracts us to Him. When we fear the LORD we take His every word seriously and we realize that He is always watching so that no sin can be committed in secret. God blesses those who learn to fear Him in this way and the fear of the LORD is one type of fear that is classified as good.

In addition to the fear of the Lord, there is another good kind of fear that God created in us to preserve life and to help us with fight or flight. When confronted with legitimate danger the adrenal glands release cortisol into the blood stream. That chemical boost jolts us with extra strength, speed and alertness enabling us to better deal with dangerous situations.

The problem comes when the elevated level of cortisol stays in our system for a long period of time. The body cannot tell the difference between real fear and fear brought on by the enemy through what the Bible calls "imaginations" (2 Cor. 10:5). And so the adrenals keep on releasing the cortisol and, over an extended period of time, the body begins to break down. Medical science has been saying for a long time that numerous diseases are stress related and stress is a form of fear.

Interestingly, our bodies contain a certain amount of cortisol even in the absence of any form of fear. For example, a "morning person" naturally has a higher level of cortisol in the morning, whereas a "night person" has a higher level at night. My friend Jim is a morning person and in the early hours he is most alert and his body temperature goes up. Another friend Phillip, on the other hand, is a night person. He is usually more alert in the evening and that is when his metabolism runs the highest. That's why he likes to stay up ridiculously late because he feels better during those hours.

While these facts are interesting, my purpose in this book is not to give a physiology lesson. What I want to communicate is there is a God-given form of fear that helps make life better and not all fear is bad. But what I will be addressing throughout this book is the type of *fear* that destroys our quality of life, rather than helping it. Unless otherwise indicated, when I use the word fear from now on it will be in reference to the destructive type of fear that is used and even initiated by the devil.

The vast majority of fear that people experience does not originate with God—it is contrary to God—it is not in alignment with His will for us. Fear in essence is believing a lie. It is the opposite of faith, peace, and love. Therefore, the person who comes to the realization that fear is sin is on the road to victory.

When I say that fear is sin I am saying that the act of coming into agreement with fear is the act of coming out of agreement with God. If I am full of fearful thinking I am not living in alignment with God's will. Once I received the revelation that fear is sin I was able to take back the ground that the enemy had gained. The reason many believers do not get lasting victory over fear is because they have never repented of it.

To further understand how fear is sin is to see fear as disobedience. I think most Christians will agree that disobedience is sin and, when I break a commandment of God, I am disobedient. When we read the scriptures we see that God has repeatedly commanded us not to fear. For example, God said to Moses, *"Be strong and of a good courage, do not fear nor be afraid of them; for the LORD your God, He is the one who goes with you. He will not leave you nor forsake you"* (Deut. 31:6). Again, He said to Joshua, *"Have I not commanded you? Be strong and of a good courage;*

*do not be afraid, nor be dismayed; for the LORD your God is with you wherever you go"* (Joshua 1:9). Therefore, it stands to reason that if I'm not obeying the Word of God, I am walking in disobedience. For this reason fear must be seen as sin.

Another reason to believe that fear is sin is found in the book of Revelation where the apostle John records the vision he received of the new heaven and the new earth. He contrasts the heirs or overcomers to those who are not allowed into heaven. *"But the **cowardly**, unbelieving, abominable, murderers, sexually immoral, sorcerers, idolaters, and all liars shall have their part in the lake which burns with fire and brimstone, which is the second death"* (Rev. 21:8, emphasis mine). Notice the other sins that cowardice (another word for fearful) is grouped with! We must understand that fear is not just weakness—it is wickedness.

If fear is sin it must be dealt with in a similar fashion as we would deal with lying, idolatry, sorcery, and adultery. We must turn from sin through repentance and renunciation because sin is contrary to the nature of God and the new nature of the believer.

Granted, this truth is not easy to swallow. One time a friend told me that worry is sin. When he spoke those words it didn't help me with my worry at all. In fact, what it did was add guilt to my life rather than help me have the peace I wanted. In retrospect, I see that my failure to understand the Father-heart of God made me unable to receive my friend's word of exhortation. One day my eyes were opened to the truth that God is for me, not against me. Therefore, when He tells me something is sin, it is because He wants the very best for my life. He has my welfare in mind.

Keep in mind that none of us can say, "I am without sin." But as I grow in Christ, though I don't become sinless, I do **sin less**. I am happy to testify that I have a lot less fear in my life than I once did but it is a process of growing into the image of Christ. I am learning to recognize fearful thoughts coming against my mind. Once I recognize them I then refuse to let them take root by resisting the devil. Scripture says, *Resist the devil and he will flee from you* (James 4:7b). I'm not batting 1000 but I am a whole lot better than I used to be. No longer am I content to allow fear a place in my life.

Never forget that just because you have a fearful thought it does not mean you have sinned. Temptation is not sin or else we are all in trouble. The Bible says that Jesus was tempted in all areas yet without sin. If He was tempted and, at the same time was without sin, then logically a temptation is not sin. A fearful thought becomes my sin when I agree with it, act upon it, entertain it, or believe it. Consequently, we must resist fearful thinking when it comes against our mind. The way Jesus resisted the devil when He was tempted in the wilderness was simply this: He quoted scripture. One of the most powerful disciplines you can incorporate into your life is scripture memory. I challenge you to commit to memory the verses on fear found in this book. Then when fear comes knocking at your door refuse to give place to it and fight it off with the Word of God. Otherwise, if you become passive, you will inevitably accept the fear as your fear. When it becomes your fear, it becomes your sin.

Fear is not only sin but I'll go a step further. The concept I am about to tell you is difficult for most Christians to grasp. Are you ready for this? Fear is a spirit. That's right! As Paul says it, "God has not given us the *spirit* of fear." To say that fear is a spirit is a notion that is foreign to our thinking and may even seem scary to some. To the contrary, it should not be frightening because in fact it is good news. If my fear is truly a spirit that means I can do something about it! I don't have to live with it any more! I can get rid of it by enforcing the victory that was won by Jesus Christ at the cross. I have witnessed saints of God instantly freed from the fear that gripped their lives when we dealt with fear as a spirit. Once a person is freed from a spirit of fear they must proactively resist the enemy when he attacks their mind lest they become enslaved again.

However, the main problem is not with resisting—it is with recognition. We usually don't see the fear that is in our lives. We don't see the culprit that is behind many of our diseases and emotional pain.

Medical science has catalogued over 3,000 different forms of fear! So fear comes in manifold sizes, shapes, and colors and it takes the Word of God and the Spirit of God to reveal the heart of man. I agree with the statement someone has made: "Deceived people don't know they are deceived. That's the nature of deception." Many people are like I was and don't see the presence of fear in their lives. Could it be that you have fear and don't even know it? Fear is dangerous to you—spirit, soul, and body—so God doesn't want you to take it lightly. If we don't deal with it there will be adverse consequences. Let me emphasize that recognition is the starting point to getting free.

Once a person gets free from a spirit of fear the battle is not over. Fearful thinking left unchecked becomes a part of a person's personality. Fear can become ingrained in our thought processes. Consequently, we need to renew our minds. Paul exhorted the Roman Christians, *And do not be conformed to this world, but be transformed by the renewing of your mind* (Romans 12:2a).

According to 2 Timothy 1:7, if you have fear you don't have a sound mind. Fear will cloud your thinking and make it so you don't think straight. Fear will also rob you of power. Fear will weaken you and neutralize your faith. If you have fear you will not be able to give and receive love to your highest potential. Therefore, treat fear for what it is—an enemy.

## Prayer

*Father in heaven, I agree with You that fear is sin. Please forgive me for coming into agreement with fear. My sin is wicked, ungodly, and against You, but now I receive Your forgiveness. The blood of Jesus cleanses me of this sin. I renounce all ungodly fear in my life and also in my generations past on both sides of my family. I ask you Lord to bring the fleshly tendency in my life to walk in fear to death at the cross of Christ. I confess the sins of my ancestors who chose to operate in fear rather than faith. I place the cross of Christ between me and the iniquity of fear that was passed onto me through my ancestors and I command fear and all its accompanying curses to be halted at the cross. And now listen to me you spirit of fear (Speak this out loud so the demon can hear you.): I command you to leave me now and go to dry places, in Jesus' name! I cancel any commitment, break any contract, and take back any territory given you through my sin of coming into agreement with you, so leave me now, in Jesus' name, Amen.*

# 2

---

# The Battle Ground

*For though we walk in the flesh, we do not war according to the flesh. For the weapons of our warfare are not carnal but mighty in God for pulling down strongholds, casting down arguments and every high thing that exalts itself against the knowledge of God, and bringing every thought into captivity to the obedience of Christ.*

*(2 Corinthians 10:3-5)*

The battleground is for the mind. Satan's mode of operation is to implant fearful thoughts into our minds hoping that we will come into agreement with fear. These "thought bombs" are aimed against us like scud missiles and explode into our thinking process, if we allow them. The Bible refers to them as "the fiery darts of the wicked."

Once God delivered me of a great amount of fear, I realized that that was only one part of the equation. As Dr. Henry Malone likes to say, "Deliverance is only one piece of the pie." I also had to replace fearful thinking with the truth. That's what the Bible calls the "renewing of your mind." We must get into the Word of God so that the Word of God will get into us.

There's a lot of truth in the old acronym, fear is **F**alse **E**vidence **A**ppearing **R**eal. These "thought bombs" from the enemy are actually lies. Jesus called Satan "the father of lies" because that's what he does best. His whole kingdom is based on a lie. In our key verse above the apostle Paul mentions strongholds. Strongholds are fortified pockets of resistance in our lives to the Spirit of God. All strongholds are based on lies and they get established in us for the purpose of bringing spiritual bondage. That's the reason Jesus said, *"You shall know the truth and the truth shall make you free."*

Janie had a stronghold that her husband was going to die at an early age. The fear of his death haunted her for the first years of their marriage. But when she began to deal with the lie, she dismantled the stronghold and this fear went away. Her father was killed in a forest fire when she was two years old, leaving her mother a widow with four young children. The enemy implanted a lie at that time of trauma in Janie's mind that she also would lose her husband at a young age.

One of my favorite fear scriptures is 2 Timothy 1:7 which states, *For God hath not given us the spirit of fear; but of power, and of love, and of a sound mind.* To have **power** means I have the strength in Christ to overcome so that I will not submit or bow down to fear. To have **love** means I love God and I know He loves me and will protect me. To have **a sound mind** means I am no longer going to think about it.

It is imperative that we take our thoughts captive to the obedience of Christ. You have to capture your thoughts. I personally had to strengthen my coping skills so that the fear wouldn't come back in. I have learned that being able to recognize where my thoughts are coming from is 90% of the battle. Since God has not given us the spirit of fear we know those kinds of thoughts don't come from Him. We also know that fear is one of the devil's favorite weapons and it directly contradicts the Word of God. So reason says that most lies come from the enemy.

Satan's lies "exalt themselves against the knowledge of God" according to our scripture passage. The "knowledge of God" as revealed throughout the Bible is that God is there to protect me. *The Lord is on my side; I will not fear: what can man do to me?* (Psalm 118:6). *I will lift up mine eyes unto the hills, from whence cometh my help? My help comes from the Lord...* (Psalm 121:1, KJV).

These "fiery darts" usually come into our minds subtly so that we are tricked into thinking they are our thoughts. When my eyes were first opened to this reality and I began to recognize these thoughts for what they were I learned how to resist them. I would say things like, "No, I'm not going to accept that lie," or "Praise God, He is my provider," or "God is on my side, I will not be afraid." To my amazement, the fears would leave when I proactively resisted them.

In addition to resisting "thought bombs," a discipline that has been invaluable to me is Christian meditation. *The psalmist declared, I will meditate on Your precepts, and contemplate Your ways. I will delight myself in Your statutes; I will not forget Your word* (Psalm 119:15-16).

What I do is get still and quiet, and sometimes I play soft contemplative music. Then I pick a scripture verse that has special meaning to me and I read that verse over and over. I pray the verse to God and ask Him to reveal the depths of meaning He has for me in the passage. I go over the verse time after time, each time focusing on a different word in the text. I ask God to implant the verse in my heart so that it will become ingrained in my very being.

If you're seeking to get free from fear, select a scripture verse that deals with that subject. Then choose a time when you will not get distracted. Turn off the phones, TV, and radio, and get quiet before the Lord. *Be still and know that I am God* (Psalm 46:10). Then turn your heart toward God. It is important that this not become a mere mental exercise. The psalmist knew the importance of meditating from the heart. *I call to remembrance my song in the night; I meditate within my heart, and my spirit makes diligent search* (Psalm 77:6).

## Prayer

*Father, in the name of Jesus, I tear down every stronghold in my life that keeps me in bondage to fear. Expose every lie I have received and replace it with Your truth. With Your help I will begin to meditate upon Your Word on a regular basis. I break every pattern of iniquity[iii] related to fear, in Jesus' mighty name, Amen.*

# 3

---

# Fear versus Peace

*"Peace I leave with you, My peace I give to you; not as the world gives, do I give to you. Let not your heart be troubled, neither let it be afraid."*

(John 14:27)

One of the opposites of fear is peace. When we learn to cultivate peace we will maintain victory over fear. One major characteristic of the Kingdom of God is peace. Paul put it this way: *For the kingdom of God is not eating and drinking, but righteousness, and **peace**, and joy in the Holy Spirit* (Romans 14:17, emphasis added). One of the nine fruits of the Spirit listed in Galatians 5:22 is peace. *But the fruit of the Spirit is love, joy, peace...* So why is it that we don't experience more peace?

We Americans live in an uptight society. Some have called it the age of anxiety. We all face situations that make us irritable and tense and that rob us of peace of mind. A major cause of heart attacks and high blood pressure is tension/stress. Every year hundreds of millions of dollars worth of tranquilizers are prescribed to shift people out of emotional overdrive.

Church members are not exempt. A dear Christian lady, who regularly attended a church I pastored, finally came to the end of her rope. One day, out of frustration and rage, she picked up a gun and shot and killed her alcoholic husband. The impact of that explosion sent shock waves throughout the community and it's a decision she will have to live with the rest of her life. One of my seminary professors committed suicide and I've witnessed many other tragedies that have rocked my spiritual equilibrium.

God's will for us is to enjoy peace of mind and tranquility of heart. The Greek word in the New Testament for peace is *eirene* and conveys the idea of harmony, the sense of rest and contentment and wholeness. That's what we all really want. Mark Twain insightfully said, "From his cradle to his grave, a man never does a single thing which has any first and foremost object save one–to secure peace of mind, spiritual comfort for himself."

Our problem is we go to the wrong places to find peace. If God created us we should find out what He says about the subject. I looked through the Bible and found passages that teach us how to experience inner peace. I found six steps.

First, **realize the source** of true peace. Jesus had a great deal to say about anxiety in Matthew 6:25-34. Why did He speak to the people of His day about this subject? Because they had trouble maintaining peace. You probably think, "How can that be? They had no freeways, traffic jams, red lights, time clocks, identity thieves, maxed out credit cards, computers crashing, or company down-sizing. They were blessed with a slower pace of life." That's the point! Peace is not based on outward circumstances.

Sometimes I feel like the blind man who was at a party. A woman asked him, "What do you do for a living?" He said, "I'm an airplane pilot for a major airline." The surprised woman inquired, "How can you do that if you're blind?" He answered, "No one knows I'm blind but it's easy. My chauffeur always picks me up and parks in the same place. I know how many steps to walk from my front door to the car and he gives me a ride to the airport. He always drops me off in the exact same spot and I know how many steps to walk to the front door and to the front desk. When I check in they assign me a co-pilot. I engage him in conversation and we walk together to the airplane. We get in the cockpit and he does the visual checks and I do the audio. At the appropriate time I have him taxi out onto the runway. Once we get clearance I push the throttle all the way forward. Then when I hear him say, 'Dear merciful God!' I pull back on the yoke." Now that's a man who lives with stress.

Look again at our key verse above. Underline the words "my peace." It's His peace. The Old Testament prophet Isaiah referred to Him as the Prince of Peace (Isaiah 9:6). Nothing ever caused Jesus to lose his peace. He exuded peace. Even while he was in a boat with His disciples and a violent storm threatened harm, he slept peacefully until they woke Him up. Never forget this important principle: Peace is a person, not a procedure. It's His peace and true peace comes from Jesus. The psalmist knew the true source of peace and wrote, *I will both lie down in peace, and sleep; for You alone, O LORD, make me dwell in safety* (Psalm 4:8).

Sure, there are practical things we must do to cultivate peace. Common knowledge dictates that we must regularly exercise as a stress reducer. Proper nutrition and adequate sleep go a long way in generating inner equilibrium. Establishing proper boundaries and learning to say "No" is essential. Don't exchange the best for the good. There are a lot of good things I can be doing. If I did all the good things that come along I would never have time to do the best and I would feel pulled in a hundred directions. In other words, keep the main thing the main thing. Ultimately true peace, everlasting inner tranquility, comes only from the author of peace who is Jesus Christ.

The second step to having peace is that we must **refocus our sight.** Isaiah the prophet wrote, *You will keep him in perfect peace, whose mind is stayed on You, because he trusts in You* (Isaiah 26:3). When we keep our eyes on the Lord we receive peace. When Peter got out of the boat, he walked on the water. But when he took his eyes off of Jesus and started to look around at the angry sea he began to sink. As long as he had his focus on Christ he was able to do the impossible. Don't keep thinking about your problems; keep your mind on the Lord.

The third step is to **recognize the secret.** It's a secret only in the sense that we are usually blinded to this important truth: God has already given us peace. Jesus said, *"My peace I give unto you."* So in reality it is ours right now, given to us as a gift. All we need to do is reach out and take what is already ours. I encourage you to take your peace. We're the ones who allow the peace to leave. That's why Jesus said: "Let not your hearts be troubled." We are the ones who "let" it happen.

The fourth step is to **rest in scripture.** The psalmist declared, *Great peace have those who love Your law, and nothing causes them to stumble* (Psalm 119:165). Jesus said, *"These things I have spoken to you, that in Me you may have peace..."* (John 16:33). The Word helps you decide your priorities. The Word brings comfort to our souls. Someone has aptly said, "A Bible that has frayed edges usually has an owner that doesn't."

I encourage scripture meditation. Meditate on a favorite Bible verse while you're going to sleep. Then that word will go over and over in your mind all night long and you will wake up with God on your mind. David said, *My soul shall be satisfied as with marrow and fatness; and my mouth shall praise You with joyful lips: When I remember You upon my bed, I meditate on You in the night watches* (Psalm 63:5-6).

The fifth step is to **rely on His sovereignty.** I jokingly say sometimes that I used to think I had to help God get the sun up in the morning. There is a lot of truth to that statement regarding the way I have tried to carry a burden that was not mine to carry. When we do that we lose our peace.

I was deeply troubled for a long time over the response one congregation had to my pastoral ministry. It used to really bother me when people I counseled didn't take heed to my words or when people didn't get saved after a clear presentation of the gospel. Then the Lord spoke to me and said, "Roger, all I ask is for your obedience; you're not responsible for the outcome."

I had fallen into the trap Satan set for me called "False Burden Bearing," a phenomenon that destroys peace every time. Once we have done our part we need to learn to let go and trust that God is faithful to do His part. The psalmist declared, *Be still, and know that I am God* (Psalm 46:10). The apostle Peter said, *Casting all your care upon Him, for He cares for you* (1 Peter 5:7).

The sixth step is to **repent of sin.** Sin robs you of peace of mind. Isaiah said, *"There is no peace," says my God, "for the wicked"* (Isaiah 57:21). You can sin, either by commission or by omission. Commission is when you do something you know God told you not to do. Omission is when you don't do what God told you to do.

For example, one time God told me to give an offering to a certain ministry. I resisted giving the money but I could get no peace until I obeyed God. After yielding to God's voice it was like a heavy load lifted off my shoulders. Other times I have expressed anger toward my wife or a friend in a way that was inappropriate. I could get no peace until I repented before God and asked their forgiveness. There are other examples but I'm sure you get the point. Sin is like having a rock in your shoe—it just won't feel right until you get it out of there.

The children of Israel got in trouble because of their repeated acts of rebellion to God. Eventually they ended up in Babylonian captivity but this was not God's perfect will for them. The Lord spoke through the prophet Jeremiah saying, *For I know the thoughts that I think toward you, says the LORD, thoughts of peace and not of evil, to give you a future and a hope* (Jeremiah 29:11). God wants us to succeed and live in peace but it is our sin that opens the door to turmoil.

## Prayer

*Lord, please reveal any sin, whether it be by commission or omission. (Listen to what the Spirit says to your heart and if there is a specific sin, confess it.) Jesus, I acknowledge that You are my peace. Forgive me for looking to people, places, or things to give me peace of mind. With Your help I will keep my eyes focused on You and I will meditate on Your Word. Thank You for the free gift of peace. I reach out and take it now, in Jesus' name, Amen.*

# 4

---

# Anxiety

*Be anxious for nothing, but in every thing by prayer and supplication, with thanksgiving, let your requests be made known to God; and the peace of God, which surpasses all understanding, will guard your hearts and minds through Christ Jesus.*

(Philippians 4:6-7)

Anxiety takes a heavy toll on the body. For example, the doctor diagnosed acid reflux disorder in my body and prescribed medication to help control it. He also advised me to put my bed on an incline so that the head was four or five inches higher than the foot of the bed. To our dismay, for the first several months, my wife and I would wake up in the morning finding ourselves at the foot of the bed. It took us a while to get used to it.

Even with these remedies the acid reflux often flared up. In my case it was extreme. After falling to sleep at night the acid would move from my stomach up into my esophagus and from there it splashed up into my lungs. The burning fire in my lungs awakened me so that I sat up almost in a state of panic. I tried to cough out the acid because it burned my lungs but each time I did the acid burned my throat all over again. I got to where I could not eat anything after 5:00pm and even then the disorder often tormented me causing loss of sleep and who knows what damage to my lungs. I knew this condition carried long-term health ramifications but I didn't know what else to do.

Fortunately, I kind of stumbled across the solution to my problem. When I began to proactively deal with fear in my life the acid reflux disorder went away. I can now eat anything, any time with no problems, praise the Lord! Not long after my healing my cousin, Robert, invited us to eat at a Brazilian restaurant at about 8:00 in the evening. The restaurant serves numerous kinds of meats and sausages as well as side dishes. They keep bringing the meat as long as you keep the green colored side of the dowel on your table facing up. When you are full you turn the red colored side of the dowel in the upward position.

My wife, Ruthie, looked at me with astonished disgust and said, "Roger, I've never seen you eat so much meat!" I'm not proud of the sin of gluttony but the good news is I went to bed shortly after that feast and didn't have a single problem with reflux. I guess you might call that the acid test.

Acid reflux is one of many anxiety disorders. Medical textbooks mention over 40 diseases that stem from anxiety and stress. Anxiety is another form of fear, and when I dealt with fear, I received my healing.

Prolonged anxiety also leads to depression. Scriptures declare, *Anxiety* (or fear) *in the heart of man causes depression, but a good word makes it glad* (Proverbs 12:25). Depression comes when we let external pressure get inside by thinking thoughts that weigh us down.[iv]

Webster's Dictionary defines anxiety as "a state of being uneasy, apprehensive, or worried about what may happen; concern about a possible future event." As all fear tends to do, it projects into the future. The Greek word *merimna* conveys this meaning: "to draw in different directions, distract, a care, especially an anxious care." ᵛ It is the same word found in 1 Peter 4:7, *Casting all your* **care** *upon him, for He cares for you.*

Again, we see confirmation that fear is sin because, if we don't cast all our care upon the Lord, we're not obeying what He told us to. I do not say this to condemn anyone but to give hope. God has a better plan than for us to live with unresolved fear that leads to disease and suffering.

Let's look carefully at Paul's admonition in Philippians 4:6-7. He says, *Be anxious for nothing.* Now if that was all he said it wouldn't help very much. Have you ever been fretting about something and someone said to you, "Don't worry?" Those words don't help very much unless they offer a solution.

Paul teaches us how to let go of anxiety. He goes on in this verse to say, *But in everything by prayer.* What he teaches is that our first response must be to go to God for His direction, strength, and peace. The Greek term *proseuchomai* is a general term for prayer, and in this context, it implies a form of worshipful acknowledgement of God and who He is. In the midst of anxiety turn your thoughts toward God. Let Him be your focus rather than your problems. The ancient prophet Isaiah said, *"You will keep him in perfect peace, whose mind is stayed on You"* (Isaiah 26:3).

The second part to Paul's admonition states, "and with supplication." To make supplication means to ask, petition, or request. At this point the believer asks God to grant specific requests. But if all you do is the first and second part of the admonition you most likely won't get free of anxiety. In fact, you probably will become more uneasy than you were before you prayed. The reason is because you are problem centered. God doesn't want us to deny negative circumstances but we must learn to glance at our problems and gaze at the Lord.

For this reason Paul adds a third part to the solution to anxiety. He says, "with thanksgiving." To pray acknowledging God and to petition is not enough. We must bathe our prayers in thanksgiving.

It's what I like to call the sandwich technique. In the Lord's Prayer Jesus taught us to begin prayer with praise and end with praise. *"Our Father which art in heaven, hallowed be thy name ... for thine is the kingdom, and the power, and the glory, for ever. Amen"* (Matthew 6:9-13). In 1 Thessalonians 5:16-18 Paul said, *Rejoice evermore. Pray without ceasing. In everything give thanks: for this is the will of God in Christ Jesus concerning you.* Again we see this pattern of sandwiching prayer between praise. Praise and thanksgiving keep you God focused. Praise gets your eyes off your problems and on to God's power.

The mark of a non-Christian is a lack of thanksgiving. In describing lost people, Paul adds, "neither were thankful." Ingratitude is listed side by side with other more obvious sins. *But fornication and all uncleanness or covetousness, let it not even be named among you, as is fitting for saints; neither filthiness, nor coarse jesting, which are not fitting, but rather **giving of thanks*** (Ephesians 5:3-4, emphasis mine). Ingratitude, then, is not just an oversight; it is wickedness. Ouch! I know that hurts.

One way to overcome anxiety is to attack your negatives in praise. The writer of Hebrews exhorted us: *By him therefore let us offer the sacrifice of praise to God continually, that is, the fruit of our lips giving thanks to his name* (Hebrews 13:15). When we obey God in this matter, the promise of God belongs to us: *And the peace of God, which surpasses all understanding, will guard your hearts and minds through Christ Jesus* (Philippians 4:7). The Greek word "guard" literally means "to keep a military guard." [vi] God's peace guards your mind from all anxiety.

Jesus said it another way. He said, *"Therefore take no thought..."* (Matthew 6:31a) or as the NIV translates it, *"So do not worry..."* It's the same Greek word Paul used in Philippians 4:6 translated as "anxious" Jesus taught that the remedy for anxiety is to seek first the Kingdom of God and his righteousness (Matthew 6:33). But the question is, "What does He mean by the term 'Kingdom of God'?"

It is the government of God—His sovereign rule. Paul defines the Kingdom of God in Romans 14:17: *For the kingdom of God is not in eating and drinking, but righteousness, and peace and joy in the Holy Spirit.* In order to obey Jesus and seek first the Kingdom we must pursue righteousness, peace, and joy in the Holy Spirit. Where is the Holy Spirit? If we are saved He lives inside us. Amazingly, Jesus also said, *"the kingdom of God is within you"* (Luke 17:20).

The righteousness of God is given to all believers as a gift. According to 2 Corinthians 5:21 we are made righteous, or placed in right standing. The righteousness, therefore, that we seek is the experiential righteousness that comes through right thinking. Bring every thought captive so that your thoughts are in keeping with God's righteousness and don't let anxious thoughts take hold of your mind. When the devil shoots those anxiety thoughts like missiles exploding in your mind, simply reject them. Just say, "No, I'm not going in that direction." Then seek after the peace and joy that comes from the Holy Spirit who is within you. This is God's antidote to anxiety.

Another helpful practice is to actually speak to your heart. The Psalmist did this. We witness this phenomenon several times in the Psalms. *Why are you cast down, O my soul? And why are you disquieted within me? Hope in God...* (Psalm 42:5a). *Bless the LORD, O my soul, and forget not all His benefits* (Psalm 103:2). *Return to your rest. O my soul, for the LORD has dealt bountifully with you* (Psalm 116:7). *Praise the LORD, O my soul* (Psalm 146:1b). David clearly spoke directly to his inner being and so can we.

Often, when I minister to others, I speak to their human spirit and tell it to be at peace. Great peace begins to settle over them and their troubled hearts begin to experience rest. Then one day I realized that I could do this to myself. I simply say something like this, "Be at peace heart; don't be troubled; don't be agitated." I have found this practice to be a tremendous help so I encourage you to try it. One of the old hymns brings inner peace as we sing the words "be still my soul."

I received an additional powerful insight from Dr. Mark Virkler, the founder and president of Christian Leadership University. He says that "emotions flow from the vision that is held before your eyes." I have seen the truth of this statement get played out in my own experience. For example, one day Ruthie didn't come home when she said she would. In fact she was about an hour late. In my mind's eye I began to see her lying beside the highway someplace as the paramedics were attending to her. Once I focused on that mental picture, my heart filled with anxiety.

I felt foolish, when shortly after that, she called to say she had stopped to do some shopping. But it demonstrated to me that emotions do indeed flow from the pictures we hold in our mind's eye. That is good news because it means that I can control my emotions by choosing which mental pictures to focus on.

Scripture teaches that we are to fix our eyes on Jesus (Hebrews 12:2). God wouldn't tell us to do so, if weren't possible for us to make a choice to focus on His Son. The Bible declares that Jesus is the Prince of Peace and an amazing thing happens when I gaze upon Him—He fills me with His peace. I have learned that I can take a Gospel story and read it slowly. As I do, I see it through the eyes of my heart. Take, for example, the story of when Jesus and His disciples were in a boat in the midst of a violent storm. Jesus was sound asleep. Finally, out of desperation they woke Him up, declaring, "Master, don't you care if this boat sinks and we perish (my paraphrase)?" Jesus stood up and simply spoke to the stormy sea, "Peace be still." And immediately the sea became as smooth as glass.

Can you see that scene through the imagination of your heart? Meditate on it until it becomes clear. You will find that as you gaze at Jesus, the Prince of Peace, He will fill you with His peace.

## Prayer

*Heavenly Father, I repent and renounce all anxiety in my life. I break any agreement I have made with anxiety and I choose to be thankful. Please forgive me Father for any lack of gratitude and right now I offer praise to You in the midst of my circumstances. You said that all things work together for good to those who love God. Thank You that You will cause good to come out of the things I'm facing. Forgive me for not seeking first Your Kingdom. I repent for focusing on my problems rather than gazing at You. In the name of Jesus Christ, the Prince of Peace, I command all anxiety to leave me now. Go to dry places and don't return, in Jesus' mighty name. I speak peace to my human spirit, Amen.*

# 5

---

# Worry

*I will bless the Lord at all times; His praise shall
continually be in my mouth. My soul shall make its boast
in the LORD: the humble shall hear of it, and be glad.
Oh, magnify the LORD with me, and let us exalt His
name together. I sought the LORD, and he heard me, and
delivered me from all my fears.*

(Psalm 34:1-4)

There is an old Greek proverb that says, "The bow that is
always bent will soon break." What that proverb seems to
be implying is that the person who is always under pressure, who
never has an opportunity to release or let go, will soon break into
a million pieces.

If there is ever a proverb that fits our society this is it. Many
people, like that bow, are strung out, full of tension, turmoil, fear,
and frustration. If I had to choose one word to summarize how
people feel today I would choose the word *worried.* Perhaps as
you're reading this book you have certain concerns on your mind.

You may be worried about terrorism, the economy or personal finances. Parents are worried about their children; children are worried about their parents. Some people worry all the time. If they are not worrying they are worried that they have nothing to worry about. Someone quipped, "Life's too short for worrying. Yes, that's what worries me."

A very tense airplane passenger began walking nervously through the terminal when stormy weather delayed his flight. While pacing back and forth he noticed a life insurance machine. It offered $250,000 in the event of death due to a plane crash. The policy was offered for just five dollars. Looking out the airport window he studied the ominous gusts of wind and began to be concerned about his family at home. For that premium it was foolish not to buy, so he purchased the coverage. With a sense of peace of mind he then searched for a place for dinner. He located a Chinese restaurant and enjoyed the good food and relaxing atmosphere. It was a good experience for him until he opened his fortune cookie. It stated, "Your recent investment will pay big dividends." I'll bet he started to worry.

Worry doesn't help. It is bad for your health. Worry takes its toll on the circulation, the heart, the endocrine system, and the whole nervous system. A day of worry is more exhausting than a day of work–it's like wrestling with an octopus. The word "worry" comes from an old Anglo-Saxon term conveying the idea of to strangle or to choke. The emotion is aptly named because it will literally choke the life out of you. One lady said, "Don't tell me it does no good to worry. Most of the things I worry about never come to pass."

Another word for worry is what I like to call "what-if-itis." "What if" projects into the future about any number of possible negative things that could happen. "What if I lose my job through down-sizing?" or "What if my husband dies at an early age?" or "What if I can't pay my bills?" or "What if my kids get into drugs?" are common examples of "what if" thoughts. Someone aptly stated,

"Worry is the advance interest you pay on troubles that seldom come." [vii]

Another side to worry relates to the past which I will call "if only" thoughts. These thoughts refer to negative events that you wish had never happened. The situation has you drawn into reliving the past and attempting to fix what went wrong. In many instances there is nothing that can be done about it. It's like trying to unscramble eggs–it can't happen. Yet emotionally, you become drained trying to solve the problem.

How do we overcome worry? Worship is the best antidote to worry. Why worry when you can worship? The worrier has his heart fixed on earthly things. The worshipper sets his heart on God and what God has done. The worrier forgets to take into account the greatness of God's power and love.

One day I was visiting my brother in northern Indiana just outside of Chesterton. That part of the country is infested with mosquitoes in the summer time. I've never seen mosquitoes that thick. My brother, some of his buddies, and I met outside in his back yard to listen to music, eat good food, and play cribbage. But these pesky bugs ate us alive. We had to constantly swat at them to keep them away.

Then one of my brother's friends showed up with a special gadget that repelled the mosquitoes. I'm not sure what it did, whether it put out a toxin or an electronic frequency, but the gadget really worked. The mosquitoes stayed away and we were free to enjoy each other's company.

Worship is a lot like that gadget. When we praise the Lord and express our adoration, the torments of the enemy seem to be repelled. Rather than expending my energy trying to swat away those pesky worrisome thoughts, I simply focus on worshipping Almighty God.

Many years ago in the early days of aviation, a man was attempting to fly around the world. Two hours into the flight and a great distance from a landing field, he heard an unusual noise coming from somewhere inside the plane. He couldn't figure it out at first but then it dawned on him that it sounded like the gnawing of a rat. Evidently a rat had gotten in at the place of departure. He began to reason, "What if the rodent is chewing through a vital cable that controls the airplane?" He knew the situation was serious and potentially fatal. Perspiration beaded up on his face and his heart raced as he realized that he was at least two hours to the nearest airport. Then the thought came to him that a rat is a mammal and as such it needs an adequate supply of oxygen to live. So he pulled back on the yoke to make the plane ascend. Higher and higher he climbed. He kept climbing until reaching over twenty thousand feet in elevation. After maintaining that altitude for several minutes the gnawing ceased. The rodent had died. It could not survive at that altitude because of the lack of oxygen. When the pilot landed safely at the nearest airport he found the dead rat.

Keep in mind that worry is like a rat. It cannot survive when we fly to the heights in praise and worship. Worry gets choked out in an atmosphere impregnated with praise! Never forget that the best antidote to worry is praise to God.

Let the words of the psalmist sink into your heart: *He who dwells in the secret place of the Most High shall abide under the shadow of the Almighty. I will say of the LORD, He is my refuge and my fortress: my God; in him will I trust. Surely He shall deliver you from the snare of the fowler, and from the perilous pestilence. He shall cover you with his feathers, and under His wings you shall take refuge; His truth shall be a shield and buckler. You shall not be afraid for the terror by night; nor for the arrow that flies by day; nor of the pestilence that walks in darkness; nor of the destruction that lays waste at noonday* (Psalm 91:1-6). I think that just about covers all of the "what if" thoughts.

When we dwell in the secret place of God through intimate worship and communion worry loses its hold on our lives. When we focus upon the greatness of God we will worship rather than worry. Worry and worship cannot dwell in the same heart for very long. They are mutually exclusive. Why? Because as we worship we begin to see that God is in control. One reason we Christians become overwhelmed is that we lose perspective of how great God is. We lose sight of the fact that we are under His care.

I want to give you permission not to worry. It is a time to express praise to God. Let's purpose to worship Him and simply refuse to worry. When your mind begins to turn toward thoughts that are worrisome, just say, "No, I'm not going that way." And then just begin to say, "Lord, I worship You, I praise You."

## Prayer

*Father in heaven, please forgive me for worrying—I recognize it as sin. I commit to worship You rather than worry. I reject and renounce all worry and I tell it to leave my life, in Jesus' name, Amen.*

# 6

## Inadequacy and Inferiority

*I have strength for all things in Christ Who empowers me—I am ready for anything and equal to anything through Him Who infuses inner strength into me, [that is, I am self-sufficient in Christ's sufficiency].*

(Philippians 4:13, AMP [viii])

Another form of fear is a feeling of inadequacy. Take a moment to read Ephesians 6:10-18. The six items of the armor of God are the belt of truth, the breastplate of righteousness, the sandals of peace, the shield of faith, the helmet of salvation and the sword of the Spirit. What distinguishes the last piece of armor from the other five items is that it is used both for defense and offense. Remember the battle is for the mind. That is why the Bible says we are to think good thoughts—thoughts of our adequacy in Christ.

The sword helps us to drive off destructive thoughts. And the Bible compares God's Word to a sword because God's Word pierces and penetrates. Hebrews 4:12 says, *For the word of God is living and powerful, and sharper than any two-edged sword, piercing even to the division of soul and spirit, and of joints and marrow, and is a discerner of the thoughts and intents of the heart.*

This verse compares God's Word to a sword, but it also teaches that the Word penetrates to every area of human personality. Jesus Himself used the sword of the Word of God during His earthly ministry. In fact, every time Jesus encountered Satan personally, the only weapon He used against him was the sword of the Spirit, or the Word of God.

Review the account of the temptation of Jesus in Matthew 4:1-11. Notice some interesting facts about this passage. First, neither Jesus nor Satan ever questioned the authority of Scripture. By the way, Jesus even quoted from the book of Deuteronomy, the one book that has been singled out for attack by many modern theologians and critics. Jesus and Satan knew the authority of Scripture.

Second, the basis of every temptation against Jesus was a temptation to doubt God's Word. That is Satan's game plan with you and me. He tries to get us to doubt what God has said. Every time the devil began with the word "if," he called something into doubt.

Third, Jesus never varied in His method of dealing with the devil. He always used the Word of God as a weapon against him. "It is written... It is written... It is also written..."

Notice that the devil can also quote Scripture. He quoted Psalm 91 but misquoted it. If the devil tried to use Scripture against Jesus, the Son of God, he will try to use it against us. That is why it is important to know your Bible and apply it accurately. You don't have to be a theologian to do that. Check the context of the immediate verses, the entire book and the overall message of the Bible. We must be careful of people who misapply Scripture and try to tempt us to go contrary to God's will.

Let's go back to Ephesians chapter six, where Paul spoke about the sword of the Spirit. See Ephesians 6:17: *And take the helmet of salvation, and the sword of the Spirit, which is the word of God.* This indicates a cooperation between the Christian and the Holy Spirit. It is a double-edged sword, the Spirit and the Word. If it is just the Word, you dry up. If it is just the Spirit, you blow up. If it is the Word and the Spirit, you grow up.

The word Paul uses for "word" is "rhema," which primarily means a spoken word. It is significant that the sword of the Spirit is not the Bible on the bookshelf or under your pillow. That does not defend your mind against the devil's attacks. But when you take the Word and quote it, relying on the Holy Spirit, it then becomes a powerful weapon.

How does this work? Let's suppose you start having thoughts of inadequacy or inferiority. Where did those thoughts come from? They didn't come from God. I call them "thought bombs." Take up the sword of the Spirit and get on the offensive and stand against them using the Word. Here is a great verse to fight off inadequacy thoughts: *I have strength for all things in Christ Who empowers me—I am ready for anything and equal to anything through Him Who infuses inner strength into me, [that is, I am self-sufficient in Christ's sufficiency]* (Philippians 4:13, AMP).

Here are some other common thought bombs: "There is nothing special about me." The truth is, I have been chosen and set apart by God. *And such were some of you. But you were washed, but you were sanctified, but you were justified in the name of the Lord Jesus and by the Spirit of our God* (1 Corinthians 6:11).

"I am inferior." The truth is, I am designed uniquely for God's purpose. *For You formed my inward parts; you covered me in my mother's womb. I will praise You, for I am fearfully and wonderfully made* (Psalm 139:13-14).

"I am not very smart." The truth is, I have God's wisdom. *But of Him you are in Christ Jesus, who became for us wisdom from God* (1 Corinthians 1:30). *Christ, in whom are hidden all the treasures of wisdom and knowledge* (Colossians 2:3).

"I have no strength." The truth is I have God's power in me. *...the exceeding greatness of His power toward us who believe, according to the working of His mighty power* (Ephesians 1:19). *"But you shall receive power when the Holy Spirit has come upon you..."* (Acts 1:8).

"I am defeated." The truth is I am victorious. *...in all these things we are more than conquerors through Him who loved us* (Romans 8:37).

When these thoughts or others come into your mind, refuse to go in that direction by declaring the Word with your mouth. Bring your thoughts into captivity to the obedience of Christ (2 Cor. 10:3-5).

# Prayer

*Father in heaven, I repent for having believed the lie that I am inadequate. Please forgive me for not believing what You say about me in Your Word. I reject and renounce all inadequacy and inferiority. I command all inadequacy and inferiority to leave me now and go to dry places, in Jesus' name, Amen.*

# 7

## Fear of Rejection

*There is no fear in love; but perfect love casts out fear, because fear involves torment. But he who fears has not been made perfect in love.*

(1 John 4:18)

Rejection represents one of the most destructive forces facing mankind. Rejection keeps you from reaching your destiny by tying you to your past. When you experience great rejection almost certainly you also deal with the fear of rejection and it is this fear that will actually connect you to more rejection. What you fear will come upon you. This explains why some people keep experiencing rejection after rejection. Herein lies the answer to why people who suffer deep rejection in their first marriage turn right around and go into another relationship filled with rejection.

John, a sixty-two year old pastor knows what rejection feels like because he experienced it at an early age. His mother and father divorced when he was yet an infant, and his father moved several thousand miles away. This was his mother's second marriage to fail. Shortly thereafter, his mother remarried for the third time. His stepfather was loud, angry, and explosive, and he feared his venomous tirades.

As a young boy growing up he received little to no nurture from him. For instance, he recalls wanting to learn to play catch with a baseball and glove. With some coaxing he finally talked his step dad into going in the back yard to play ball. The step dad had him stand in front of the cinder block wall and proceeded to burn it in. The hard ball hurt John's hand even through the glove and so he started jumping to the side when he threw his fastball. That only infuriated the step dad and he began to call John a sissy. His favorite term was "panty-waist," and John determined from that point on to avoid contact with him, if possible.

Neither John nor his siblings ever heard him say that he loved them. Later, after the kids were grown, his step dad changed and never forgot to tell the adult children he loved them every time they visited their parents, and for that John is grateful. But the damage had already been done.

Another factor that deepened the rejection was that his mother had children from each of her three marriages. His two older sisters' last name was Johnson, his three younger siblings were Merriman and he was the only child with his last name. It always hurt when friends would ask him why his name was different. Keep in mind that when he grew up in the 1950's, rarely did you see couples get divorced, remarried, and living in blended families.

He also felt like he didn't get his parents approval unless he performed. If he brought home a report card with all A's and B's, his parents never gave him praise for doing a good job. Instead, he heard them say, "Next time bring home all A's." A performance-based home breeds rejection and fear of rejection.

To make matters worse, his stepfather did not make a lot of

money as a construction worker and it proved difficult to feed and clothe a family of eight. Consequently, the children often attended school dressed in raggedy hand-me-downs and shoes with holes or flapping soles. Needless to say, John received a lot of ridicule from his classmates, which added to the overall feeling of rejection.

Rejection devalues people and strikes a devastating blow to one's self-esteem. The noun "rejection" comes from the verb "to reject." Webster's Dictionary defines "reject" as to refuse to take, to discard or throw out as worthless, useless, or substandard; cast off or out; to pass over or skip; to deny acceptance, care, love, etc. We have all received rejection from one degree to another, and none of us likes it.

If your school classmates ever called you names you have experienced rejection. If you have ever been picked last when they were choosing teams you know rejection. If you have ever been ignored, persecuted, maligned, made fun of, betrayed, abandoned, abused, forgotten, or overlooked, then you know what rejection is about. Of course some acts of rejection hurt more deeply than others.

Beloved, if you have experienced deep rejection then probably you possess the fear of rejection. Because rejection hurts so badly, we naturally want to avoid it at all costs and, consequently, we develop a fear of it. Tragically, however, the fear of rejection in our lives will act as a magnet to draw more rejection to ourselves. That is why we must not tolerate it for one minute. We must fight it with everything we have.

When a person fears rejection that person tends to twist and misinterpret what other people say and do. For example, when a husband comes home from work and he says to his stay-at-home wife, "Honey, what did you do today?" Rejection in her will hear him say, "You lazy thing, why didn't you do something more constructive with your time?" Or your pastor walks right by a member at church. The truth may be that he is in a hurry to get something ready before the service starts but they interpret it to mean that they're not appreciated and it might be a good idea to start looking for another church. Rejection causes a person to be easily offended so other people have to watch what they say around them.

When a person suffers from fear of rejection they will have a hard time feeling accepted. Even when others express sincere love they can't receive it. They always search for approval from people around them but never feel like they fully receive it.

A person who fears rejection will often reject others. In their minds, it is less painful to reject than to be rejected. When I was a young man the custom was when boys had a special girlfriend, it was called "going steady." Giving the girl your ring to be worn on a chain around her neck marked the relationship. I'm sure I broke those girls' hearts because I always broke up with them before they could break up with me. That's fear of rejection!

I am learning that fear of rejection sometimes leads to physical problems such as asthma and allergies. My wife, Ruthie, had severe food allergies as well as allergies to pollens and grass. Ingesting the least little bit of corn products would send her immediately to the restroom to vomit. If you have ever read the ingredients of packaged foods you have realized that corn is in most packaged food we eat. It is even used to sweeten soft drinks and desserts.

Early in our marriage I began to beg God to heal her. One day, after intense prayer, the Lord spoke to me and said, "I've already healed her." With my denominational background, I didn't comprehend what God was saying. I asked, "Lord if you healed her why is she so sick?" So over the years she continued to suffer and her diet became more and more restricted.

Then one day, after studying about the effects of fear and rejection,

I ministered deliverance to her in this area. After we received this revelation, we saw that she possessed a great deal of fear of rejection. We discovered that this fear came into her life through the fear of abandonment. (Fear of abandonment is a form of the fear of rejection.) Her father was killed when she was a little girl. Through this tragedy the devil set up a stronghold of fear.

Once she saw the truth of the matter, we dealt with and cast out the fear of rejection. To our amazement, almost immediately all of her allergies went away. She doesn't even need to take antihistamines for air-borne allergens. She can eat as much corn on the cob or popcorn as she desires. Praise the Lord! Jesus had already healed her over 2,000 years ago on the cross, but the fear of rejection was blocking her healing from being manifested.

Please understand that you do not have to live with the fear of rejection! The Good News is that Jesus bore our rejection. In Isaiah 53:3-4a we read, *He is despised and rejected of men, a Man of sorrows and acquainted with grief. And we hid, as it were, our faces from Him; He was despised, and we did not esteem him. Surely he has borne our griefs and carried our sorrows.* Jesus knows how rejection feels but He carried it away when He died for us on the cross.

God does not reject us. Let the words of the apostle Paul sink into your hearts, *According as he hath chosen us in him before the foundation of the world, that we should be holy and without blame before him in love: Having predestinated us unto the adoption of children by Jesus Christ to himself, according to the good pleasure of his will, To the praise of the glory of his grace, wherein he hath made us accepted in the beloved* (Ephesians 1:4-6).

He accepts us! When I got the revelation that God accepts me it took the sting away that others rejected me. Rejection still hurts but it is not devastating. You say, "God will accept me if I measure up, if I do those things that please Him." No! The Good

News is that God made me completely righteous when I gave my heart to Christ. *For he hath made him to be sin for us, who knew no sin; that we might be made the righteousness of God in him* (2 Corinthians 5:21). God has made me righteous as a free gift just because I received His Son. God sees me as having kept the entirety of the law since the day I was born. That's Good News!

The most powerful exercise that we can do to free ourselves from the devastating impact of rejection is to soak in God's acceptance. That's why the apostle John said, *There is no fear in love; but perfect love casts out fear, because fear involves torment. But he who fears has not been made perfect in love* (1 John 4:18).

Take time meditating on the great love that God has for you. Spend time in His presence soaking in His love. Play worshipful music, get in a relaxed position and begin thanking God for His love. Hear Him say that you are accepted, you are forgiven, you are righteous, and that He will never forget you because you are the apple of His eye.

Here are some more scriptures to ponder: *"Can a woman forget her nursing child, and not have compassion on the son of her womb? Surely they may forget, yet will I not forget you. See, I have inscribed you on the palms of my hands; your walls are continually before Me"* (Isaiah 49:15-16). *I will praise You, for I am fearfully and wonderfully made; marvelous are Your works, and that my soul knows very well. My frame was not hidden from You, when I was made in secret, and skillfully wrought in the lowest parts of the earth. Your eyes saw my substance, being yet unformed. And in Your book they were all written, the days fashioned for me, when as yet there were none of them. How precious also are Your thoughts to me, O God! How great is the sum of them! If I should count them, they would be more in number than the sand; when I awake, I am still with You* (Psalm 139:14-18).

# Prayer

*Heavenly Father, I repent and renounce coming into agreement with fear of rejection. Being rejected is not sin but when I received that fear I sinned against You. Now I receive Your forgiveness and Your cleansing by the blood of Jesus. You spirit of fear of rejection, I address you in Jesus' name. I command you to leave me now and go to dry places. I cancel any commitment, break any contract, and take back any territory given you through my sin of receiving fear of rejection. And now Father in Heaven, please help me to recognize when the fear of rejection is coming against me and give me grace to refuse to accept it, in Jesus' name, Amen.*

# 8

---

# Fear of Abandonment

*Let your conduct be without covetousness; be content with such things as you have. For He Himself has said, "I will never leave you nor forsake you." So we may boldly say: "The LORD is my helper; I will not fear. What can man do to me?"*

(Hebrews 13:5-6)

M y father and mother divorced when I was still an infant. I lived with my mother on the West Coast, while my father moved to Indiana nearly, 2,000 miles away. I never saw him again until I was around five years old. I was too young when he left us to have expressed visible sorrow or mourning, yet in my spirit, I no doubt sensed his absence and experienced an inner wound. Out of the trauma of divorce the devil planted fear of abandonment in my heart.

The enemy watered that seed every chance he had. When I was five years old I took a train trip with my grandparents from California to New York and back. During a stop at the depot in Chicago I got separated from grandma and grandpa. Imagine the panic of a five-year-old in a strange place with hundreds of people around me I'd never seen before. As I searched for them in the crowded train station the fear of abandonment grew stronger inside me. Thankfully, a policeman found me and helped me reunite with my grandparents; nevertheless, more damage had been done.

Fear of abandonment opens us up to various diseases including asthma and Hodgkin's disease. Studies have indicated that children of one-parent families are more prone to asthma.[ix] We were not created to live in a sustained sense of fear, so fear in any form will eventually take its toll on the body.

My close friend, Rachel, lost her father when she was age two. He was killed fighting a forest fire and left a wife and four children to fend for themselves. His death wounded her little two-year-old heart and the seed of fear of abandonment was sown by the enemy. For years she suffered from multiple food allergies until she dealt with the fear of abandonment. Once she did the allergies disappeared over night.

When Joshua was getting ready to lead the children of Israel into the Promised Land he must have experienced great fear. Otherwise, the Lord would not have exhorted him three times in one chapter to, *"Be strong and of good courage"* (Joshua 1:6-7, 9). But God knew that simply commanding Joshua not to fear would not have been enough to help him be courageous. He went on to say, *"I will never leave you nor forsake you"* (Joshua 1:5), and *"The LORD your God is with you wherever you go"* (Joshua 1:9). Just knowing God is right there with us tends to relieve our fears and fill us with courage.

Even though our earthly guardians abandon us, whether knowingly or unknowingly, Jesus will never leave our side. Whatever you've been through, God's eyes have always been upon you. *"Can a woman forget her nursing child, and not have compassion on the son of her womb? Surely they may forget, yet I will not forget you. See, I have inscribed you on the palms of my hands; your walls are continually before Me"* (Isaiah 49:15-16).

In the Twenty Third Psalm notice the reason David gave for not fearing evil even during the very worst circumstances. *Yea, though I walk through the valley of the shadow of death, I will fear no evil; for **You are with me*** (Psalm 23:4, emphasis mine). No matter what we face, God is with us.

One reason He will never abandon us is because He is our heavenly Father. Paul said, *For you did not receive the spirit of bondage again to fear, but you received the Spirit of adoption by whom we cry out, Abba, Father. The Spirit Himself bears witness with our spirit that we are children of God* (Romans 8:15-16).

Consider that Paul writes this epistle to the Christians living in Rome, and the background to the adoption procedure in that culture is significant. By adoption, someone who was not related by blood became a member in the family, receiving a new father. The tie was stronger than with some of the other family kin or descendants, and in the eyes of the law, the adopted person was born again into the new family. In a legally binding way the individual received a new father and became the heir of his father's estate. If other sons were subsequently born, who were blood relatives, the adopted son could not lose his rights as a son.

The adoption procedure was transacted in the presence of seven witnesses. If the father died and there was a dispute over the adopted son's right to the inheritance, then one or more of the original seven witnesses stepped forward. They were called on to verify that the adoption was genuine. In the same way, the Holy Spirit is the witness that we were adopted into God's family.

Not only are we adopted but the Bible says we are actually born into the family of God. Abba means "one who is birthed from his loins." Abba is a term of endearment meaning "daddy" or "papa." As a Christian I can confidently say, "God is my daddy."

Our earthly fathers may fail and abandon us through death, disease, divorce, or drunkenness, but the good news is that our Father in heaven perfectly and faithfully watches over His children. He will never leave us nor forsake us. He promised it and He cannot lie.

## Prayer

*Thank You, Father, for Your promise that You will never leave me nor forsake me. Thank You that You are always faithful. I reject and renounce all fear of abandonment. I command this fear to leave me now, in the name of Jesus, Amen.*

# 9

---

# Fear of Another's Words

*For I hear the slander of many; fear is on every side;
while they take counsel together against me, they scheme
to take away my life. But as for me, I trust in You, O
LORD: I say, "You are my God." My times are in Your
hand; deliver me from the hand of my enemies, and from
those who persecute me.*

(Psalm 31:13-15)

Any time you step out in obedience to God's call and direction
you run the risk of being misunderstood, even by close
friends and family. People are usually down on what they're not
up on. When they don't understand what you're doing they will
often reject you because you got out of the box they painted for
your life.

When Bill first got saved his life was radically changed. He
experienced joy, peace, and meaning in life that he had not known
before. When he shared his testimony with his best "friend," he
thought he had gone off the deep end and didn't want to have
anything to do with him. Bill was unwavering in his commitment
to Christ but that is not to say his "friend's" rejection did not hurt.

It hurts when people judge, criticize, condemn and gossip about us. Because of the pain, we may develop a fear of people's negative words. But when we give in to this deadly fear it inhibits us from being all God wants us to be.

Bill experienced this very phenomenon. After hearing his "friend's" negative words, he tried to avoid situations that would cause him similar pain. Consequently, out of fear, he kept his newfound faith to himself at his work place. He knew that the "guys" were quick to judge people who were different from the crowd. Finally one day a co-worker confronted him about a rumor he had heard that Bill had become a Christian. Meekly he admitted to it only to hear his condemning words, just as Bill had feared.

God directed the prophet Ezekiel to deliver a message of impending judgment upon the Jewish people. No one wants to hear a message that they've been wrong and, apparently, Ezekiel became fearful of the people's reaction. God addressed his fear. *"And you, son of man, do not be afraid of them nor be afraid of their words, though briers and thorns are with you, and you dwell among scorpions; do not be afraid of their words or dismayed at their looks, though they are a rebellious house"* (Ezekiel 2:6).

Notice that along with the fear of people's words comes the fear of their facial expressions. Non-verbal language can communicate more powerfully a person's judgment and criticism than their actual words.

If Ezekiel had given in to his fears he would no longer have been able to serve as a prophet and we would not have a book of the Bible with his name. Fear of another's words will rob you of your destiny and effectiveness in the work of the Kingdom.

Peter lost his credibility for the Kingdom when he, out of fear of criticism, denied the Lord three times. But something radically changed Peter. After the day of Pentecost, when God poured out the Holy Spirit on the church, Peter became a new man. Rather than cowering back from confrontation he boldly proclaimed the gospel. To give us boldness is part of the ministry of the Holy Spirit. After His resurrection Jesus instructed the disciples: *But ye shall receive power, after that the Holy Ghost is come upon you: and ye shall be witnesses unto me both in Jerusalem, and in all Judea, and in Samaria, and unto the uttermost part of the earth* (Act 1:8, KJV).

## Prayer

*Father in heaven, I repent for having come into agreement with the fear of people's negative words of judgment, criticism, and condemnation. Please forgive me for not trusting You in this area of my life. Fear of another's negative words, I command you to leave me now, in the name of Jesus and go to dry places. Father, I ask You to give me a fresh infilling of the Holy Spirit so that I will not be afraid to boldly proclaim Your word, in Jesus' name, Amen.*

# 10

---

# Fear of Bad News

*Surely he will never be shaken; the righteous will be in everlasting remembrance. He will not be afraid of evil tidings; his heart is steadfast, trusting in the LORD. His heart is established, he will not be afraid, until he sees his desire upon his enemies.*

(Psalm 112:6-8)

R oy went through a season in his life when nothing seemed to work. His finances got so bad and his income dried up to the extent that he was broke. His home-based business generated income on the basis of commission-only sales. When he sold, he made money. When he didn't sell, he worried about how to pay the mortgage and other bills, let alone groceries. For months nothing clicked.

To make matters worse, his money came in the form of an advance. Most of his clients opted to pay a monthly premium. If, after purchasing his service, they decided to cancel and the business didn't stay on the books for eight full months, he had to return all the paid commission to the company. With this system, he never knew how much money he actually had.

Perhaps the economy played a role, but week after week he received calls from customers wishing to cancel. Every time he got a phone call his heart sank. "Oh no, who is going to cancel now," he complained to his wife when the phone rang. At this point he had opened his heart to another form of fear, the fear of bad news.

Most people don't realize how commonly this form of fear presents itself in our society. It's like the man who didn't want to go to the doctor for a check up for fear that the doctor might find something wrong. Human reason says this kind of behavior is silly because it may lead to more serious problems down the road. But fear is not rational. It comes from the heart.

Denise and her husband were struggling financially and staying on top of the bills proved challenging. Every time a new bill arrived in the mail Denise threw it in a pile of other unopened mail she was avoiding. Out of fear she refused to even look at the invoices. Obviously this coping mechanism didn't work.

The word "steadfast" in the key verses for this chapter conveys great meaning. A steadfast heart exudes peace even in the midst of trial. The psalmist uses the same Hebrew word in another place: *I am in the midst of lions; I lie among ravenous beasts—men whose teeth are spears and arrows, whose tongues are sharp swords. Be exalted, O God, above the heavens; let your glory be over all the earth. They spread a net for my feet—I was bowed down in distress. They dug a pit in my path—but they have fallen into it themselves. My heart is steadfast O God, my heart is* **steadfast**... (Psalm 57:4-7a, NIV[x], emphasis mine).

When we look at the context for the key verses we make an interesting discovery. Notice the verses surrounding Psalm 112:6-8. *Good will come to him who is generous and lends freely* (Psalm 112:5, NIV) and immediately following we read, *He has scattered abroad his gifts to the poor* (Psalm 112:9a, NIV). The context has to do with giving.

Another amazing truth is that the apostle Paul quotes this passage in 2 Corinthians 9:9, his great treatise on the subject of giving. Then what is God saying to us? He teaches that there is something about a life style of giving that insulates us from the destructive nature of bad news.

How can that be? When I sow seed into Kingdom work I am making a statement that everything I have comes from God. When Roy finally reminded himself that God is his source, not his clients, then great peace flooded his heart.

The psalmist confidently stated, *The LORD is on my side; I will not fear: what can man do unto me* (Psalm 118:6)? Giving releases the hold you have on your life and destiny. It's saying, "God, I trust you to take care of me."

One way to fight fear is to go after it with an opposite spirit. The spirit of sacrificial generosity deals a blow to the fear of bad news. Maybe you've never seen this connection but meditate on Psalm 112 and let God speak to your heart.

## Prayer

*Father in heaven, I repent and renounce coming into agreement with the fear of bad news. I sinned against You but now I receive Your forgiveness. By Your grace I will be a cheerful giver of my resources. Fear of bad news, I reject you, I renounce you and I command you to leave me now, in Jesus' name, Amen.*

# 11

## The Fear of Death

*Inasmuch then as the children have partaken of flesh and blood, He also himself likewise shared in the same, that through death He might destroy him who had the power of death, that is, the devil, and release those who through fear of death were all their lifetime subject to bondage.*

(Hebrews 2:14-15)

E lisabeth Kubler-Ross blazed the trail in developing therapy for the terminally ill, including children. She told the story of an eight-year-old boy who was dying with an inoperable brain tumor. The child was urged to draw pictures to help him express his feelings about dying. In one picture he drew the background consisting of the sun, trees, a house, grass, and a huge army tank that stood in the foreground. A tiny figure was in front of the gigantic gun barrel with a stop sign in his hand. That's the way the child felt—helpless in the face of death. His protests could do nothing to stop the onslaught of death.[xi]

For many people the reality of death terrifies them more than anything else. The devil's chief weapon over mankind is fear, especially the fear of death. Satan seeks to bring people into slavery and, as a slave master, he uses a whip as a means of power and control. The devil's whip is fear of death, the king of terrors, and he uses it to gain control over the lives of people.

My grandmother was a godly woman but the fear of death got the best of her. Prior to WWII, she and my grandfather were living on a farm in Wisconsin with their children where they experienced bitter cold weather every winter. Somehow my grandmother got it in her mind that if she had to endure another winter in that climate she would surely die.

So they put their home up for sale hoping for a buyer. As spring turned into summer and no one made an offer they drastically reduced the asking price. Still no buyers expressed interest. They lowered the price more and more as fall approached until, in desperation, they practically gave the house and land away and moved to the west coast.

By this time the little money they had from the sale of their home ran out and the family was reduced to living in the squalor of a shantytown work camp. My mother, a teenage girl at the time, seeking a way to survive, married a young man she had just met and barely knew. The marriage proved disastrous as her husband revealed his true colors of abusive behavior.

Do you see what fear can do? The devil uses it to cause us to make poor decisions. Because of the fear of death my grandmother made poor decisions that led to spiritual, psychological, economic, and marital death.

When sin entered into the world in the Garden of Eden death became the most certain fact of life. Through original sin the devil had the power of death given to him and he became the father of death. The New Testament refers to him as Beelzebub

(Luke 11:18-19), the name meaning the lord of the flies. What do flies do? They are drawn to that which is dead or dying. Satan is attracted to death and seeks to bring death.

Satan's kingdom is one of darkness and death (Colossians 1:13), and Jesus, in speaking of the devil said, *"The thief cometh not, but for to steal, and to kill, and to destroy: I am come that they might have life, and that they might have it more abundantly"* (John 10:10). Simply put, Jesus brings life; the devil brings death. Jesus also referred to the devil as "a murderer" and the "father of lies" (John 8:44). Because sin brings death (Romans 6:23), in this sense, Satan exercises power in the realm of death.

The New Testament affirms that Jesus came to destroy the works of the devil (1 John 3:8b). The Amplified Version reads, *The reason the Son of God was made manifest (visible) was to undo (destroy, loosen, and dissolve) the works the devil [has done].* According to our key verse, Hebrews 2:14-15, Jesus came to destroy him that had power of death, that is, the devil. The word "destroy" does not mean "annihilate." Obviously, Satan is still alive and well on planet earth and very active. The word in the Greek conveys the idea of "rendering ineffective, inoperative, or impotent." Perhaps a better way to translate the word is not "destroyed" but "disarmed."

How did Jesus disarm him? The only way to disarm the devil was to rob him of his chief weapon, death. To take away this weapon, Jesus experienced death. Doesn't it seem ironic that it took death to destroy death? Jesus went into the very throes of death and came out on the other side through the resurrection, thus defeating death. You see, the devil's chief weapon was death but God's chief weapon is more powerful. It's the power of the resurrection. Death couldn't keep Jesus in the grave because the Spirit of God raised him back to life.

This is a message of good news for us. The apostle Paul asserted, *But if the Spirit of him that raised up Jesus from the dead dwell in you*... (Romans 8:11a). Think of it! The same Spirit that raised Jesus from the dead dwells in you. Jesus could say, *"Because I live, ye shall live also"* (John 14:19c).

Physical death no longer has power over me because I will live again. If the worst thing happens to me and I am killed it's not really a bad thing at all. I am immediately ushered into the presence of God. I can say with Paul, *For to me to live is Christ, and to die is gain* (Philippians 1:21), and *"O death, where is your sting? O Hades, where is your victory?"* (1 Corinthians 15:55).

If Jesus rose again, I will rise again–this is victory. *But thanks be to God, who gives us the victory through our Lord Jesus Christ* (1 Corinthians 15:57).

## Prayer

*Heavenly Father, please forgive me for bowing down to the kingdom of darkness by allowing the fear of death to have a place in my life. Thank you, Father, for forgiving me. The blood of Jesus cleanses me now of the sin of coming into agreement with the fear of death. Fear of death, I reject you, I renounce you and I break any agreement I made with you. Jesus came to undo, destroy, loosen, and dissolve the works the devil has done. Therefore, in Jesus' name, I command you to leave me now. The same Spirit that raised Jesus from the dead dwells in me, and because Jesus lives, I will live with God forever. Amen.*

# 12

---

# Panic Attacks

*Do not be afraid of sudden terror, nor of trouble from the wicked when it comes; for the LORD will be your confidence, and will keep your foot from being caught.*
(Proverbs 3:25-26)

Perhaps you sometimes feel as if you are having a heart attack because your heart races and pounds in your chest, you have heaviness around the sternum, and you experience dizziness and lightheadedness. Fearfully, you rush to the emergency room thinking you might die. But after thorough tests the results show that nothing is wrong with your heart. If these symptoms sound familiar, you may be suffering from panic attacks.[xii]

Sometimes those who have this condition think they are about to lose control of themselves and do something weird, so that they will be made to look foolish in front of other people. These individuals often believe that they are going crazy. Panic attack sufferers may also feel like they are gasping for air and end up hyperventilating because they fear that they will suffocate from lack of oxygen. They may experience flushes, chills, jumpiness, trembling, twitching muscles, sweaty palms, flushed face, and tingling in the hands, feet, legs, and arms. If you experience these symptoms, by all means, seek medical help.

If you live with panic attacks you are not alone. The National Institute of Mental Health approximates that at least four million Americans suffer from panic attacks. A number of experts feel that this is a low estimate because many victims never receive the proper diagnosis.[xiii] In any year 2.4 million Americans suffer from panic disorder.[xiv]

Carlos feared getting stuck in a traffic jam. When the freeway came to a standstill, the terror of being trapped overwhelmed him. Thoughts of jumping out of the car and sprinting for a place of refuge rushed through his mind. Then his mind ran wild as an internal argument ensued regarding the absurdity of wanting to run. Beads of sweat trickled down his reddened face and his knuckles whitened as he anxiously gripped the steering wheel. He sensed he was viewing the cars in front him as though he were looking through a tunnel. Consequently, he thought he must be having a nervous breakdown. The idea of going crazy produced even more anxiety. Then, when the car in front of him edged forward, he found solace in the realization that he would soon be home.

The symptoms may vary from person to person but Carlos was not going crazy. He was perfectly healthy. He was simply experiencing a panic attack. Freeway traffic tended to trigger his malady. For other people, triggers include being in a crowded store or in an elevator or on an airplane. On the other hand, and unlike Carlos' story, Dr. Thomas A. Richards states, "Panic is not necessarily brought on by a recognizable circumstance, and it may remain a mystery to the person involved. These attacks come 'out of the blue.' At other times, excessive stress or other negative life conditions can trigger an attack."[xv]

For Carlos, the panic attacks typically lasted from two to eight minutes. Other individuals with more severe attacks may experience a series of incidents of increases and decreases of symptoms every few minutes until they end by complete exhaustion and sleep. Panic disorder typically strikes in young adulthood. Approximately half of all people who have panic disorder develop the condition before age twenty-four.[xvi]

Without treatment, Carlos' condition could easily progress to what is called panic disorder with agoraphobia. If he gets to the place where he dreads the thought of getting on a freeway for fear that he might have another panic attack, he is developing panic disorder. At this stage he may do everything possible to avoid freeway driving. Eventually the pattern of avoidance may lead him to the point where he is unable to drive at all or even step out of his house.

This phenomenon relates to the key verse above where the Bible says, *Be not afraid of sudden terror.* In other words, don't be afraid of fear. It is the fear of fear that locks in the original fear. It's like a snowball effect. The more Carlos fears the fear, the more fear he will have, which in turn creates more fear and so on.[xvii]

However, if you suffer from panic attacks or panic disorder don't be discouraged. The National Institutes of Mental Health says that they are "some of the most successfully treated psychological problems." Therapy from a knowledgeable therapist helps over ninety percent of panic patients.[xviii] Through cognitive-behavioral therapy some relief may be noticed within six to eight weeks.

But are there some other practical things Christians can do to gain victory? The place to start in dealing with panic is with the body. We begin here because that's where much of the problem lies. When a sudden onset of fear occurs the body releases adrenaline (epinephrine) which prepares a person for strenuous physical activity. The release of adrenaline increases the heart rate and leads to perspiration and hyperventilation. Because major activity rarely happens, rapid breathing leads to a reduction in the level of carbon dioxide. This results in a change in the blood pH, leading to other symptoms such as numbness, tingling, or dizziness. Heavy breathing or hyper-ventilation can exacerbate the symptoms of a panic attack. Sadly, the individual experiencing the panic usually is not cognizant of this progression and consequently, sees these symptoms as confirmation that the condition is serious. This realization in turn fuels more intense physical symptoms and psychological distress.

Therefore, the best first response is to deal with your body. Learn to go limp like a rag doll. Imagine a rag doll. When you move it the arms and legs just swing about without a bit of tension. Let your entire body go limp as much as possible. In some settings you can't do this but if, for example, you are standing in an elevator let the top half of your body relax. When anxiety leads to the release of adrenaline our body and muscles tighten up because we are being prepared for action. Don't fight the fact that your body is experiencing fear—just go limp.

The next physical response is to breathe deeply from your diaphragm. People suffering from panic attacks tend to breathe from their chest. But it is generally considered a healthier and fuller way to consume oxygen to breath from the diaphragm. If you breathe correctly it really does reduce tension and anxiety.

Someone once told me to imagine two nostrils just below my belly button. That practice has helped me learn to breathe diaphragmatically. Another beneficial exercise for me was placing a book on my stomach as I lay in bed. If the book went up and down I was breathing from my diaphragm. Take long, slow intakes of air and exhale through pursed lips. Every time you sense anxiety coming on, first go limp and then breathe deeply from your diaphragm.

Before we can deal with the spiritual dynamic of panic attacks we need to lower the stress level so we can focus on truth. The body is easiest to deal with in the beginning of deliverance for the purpose of lowering our stress level. When the stress level is lowered through ministering to the body we become more able to listen to the strategy to get free. Until the stress level is reduced, the ability of the mind to focus is limited by self-focus.[xix]

The next step is to address the soul. One aspect of the human soul is our mind or our thoughts. Certain thoughts lead to anxiety so the key is to "bring our thoughts into captivity" (2 Corinthians 10:3-5). This means that we must stop the thoughts that lead to anxiety and replace them with thoughts of peace. Your brain chemistry will actually change as a result of changing your thoughts.

When anxious thoughts bombard your mind the first thing to do is to say, "No, I'm not going to go that way. These thoughts are not from God." Then, here are some possible statements to make out loud:

1. I'm just going to relax and be calm because God is with me. He says He will never leave me nor forsake me. (Hebrews 13:5).

2. So what if I feel some anxiety right now? I can do all things through Christ who strengthens me. (Philippians 4:13).

3. Right now I'm having anxious thoughts. They will soon pass. It's only temporary.

4. So what if I make a fool out of myself? It is no big deal because God still loves me. Nothing can separate me from His love. (Romans 8:38-39).

5. I'm not really going crazy. That's just a lie. In Christ I

have a sound mind. (2 Timothy 1:7).

6. I'm not going to fight my feelings because I am aware that feelings come and feeling go. Instead, I accept my feelings of peace that Jesus gave me (John 14:27).

Another effective tool in renewing your thoughts is to go to a Biblical story and replay the scene in your mind as though you are watching a movie. Do this exercise when you feel panic and anxiety beginning to rise up. For example, after relaxing your body and breathing deeply, go to the story in the New Testament that deals with Jesus calming the stormy sea (Mark 4:35-41). Go over this passage until you can see an instant replay in your mind's eye. You may have another favorite story and that is fine. Just remember that refocusing your thoughts on Jesus creates peace because true peace comes from Him.

Here is what Olen Griffing, former pastor of Shady Grove Church and current leader of Antioch Oasis International network of churches, has to say in this regard:

> *"It is through ministry to one's soul that the legal access the enemy has had to the mind is closed. Sometimes this has to do with simply not knowing who they are in Christ. Sometimes it may have to do with something historical in their life that triggers thoughts that give rise to anxiety. It could also have to do with a lack of confidence that they are loved by the Lord. Basically, most people have been led to believe a lie that is straight from the pit of hell. To me it is important for a person to see that dealing with the body and then the soul has one objective, to be so healed that the enemy has no topography to hold on to."* [xx]

After you have addressed the body and soul (mind), next you need to address the spirit of fear behind the panic attacks. Make sure to read this book in its entirety and pray the prayers at the end of each chapter because this will give you a handle on how to deal with the spiritual dynamic. My recommendation at this point is to read the rest of the book and then revisit this chapter if you suffer from panic attacks or panic disorder.

I close this chapter with the personal testimony of Olen Griffing. From his story I pray that you will find hope in knowing that God has freedom for you.

*"When I was twenty-two while driving alone in the Texas plains one evening, I experienced real terror. It was sudden and I had no warning. I became deathly afraid of something, but I did not know of what or whom to be afraid. I pulled into Benjamin, a small Texas town, and immediately drove myself to their one and only small hospital. I knew there had to be something wrong with my body. After two days I was released with a diagnosis of dehydration, but it was just the beginning of nineteen years of pure terror.*

*"Before that day in Benjamin, Texas, I had only three memories of inappropriate fear. As a seven-year-old child, I had a few night time bouts with being unusually afraid. Then again, when I was ten, while living in Ballenger, Texas, I had the same feelings. At the time I thought these feelings were somewhat normal. Mother took me to the doctor and he told her to give me warm milk before going to bed with the promise that it would help. The last episode of fear that I had in my early years was as a senior in high school. That lasted for just a few minutes and was soon forgotten. After all, I was a young man with nothing to fear. In fact, I was convinced that these kinds of feelings of fear were not manly.*

*"After graduating from high school and taking a few hours of college at a local school, I spent some time in the U.S. Army. Then I worked at odd jobs just long enough to get accepted to the Texas Department of Public Safety Law Enforcement Academy in Austin, Texas. Upon successfully graduating I became a patrolman. It was while driving to*

*my first assignment that I had the first real panic attack described in the opening paragraph. For the next eight years as a patrolman I was sure that I had heart disease, brain cancer, or some other terrible malady that the doctors could not find.*

*"During this time I visited the emergency room numerous times only to hear that the doctors thought I was hypoglycemic or had a stomach ulcer. Surely someone, I thought, had an answer to my fear, but the doctors had no answers. I got to the place where I was afraid to be alone. I would regularly feel my pulse, taking my own heart rate in an unobtrusive way so no one would notice. I would watch the color of my tongue and my finger nails to make sure they weren't too blue. I noticed that I experienced muscle twitching in different parts of my body that was quite annoying. I could be feeling well one moment then suddenly it was as if a blanket of fear would descend on me. It would come with a thought like, 'Something is wrong.' Then I would say to myself, 'Oh, no! Not again.'*

*"On top of all this I would begin feeling very disoriented, like I was living in a bubble and felt as if I could not connect with anyone around me. I would get lightheaded with tingling in my extremities. I would feel like I couldn't breathe well. Then my heart would begin to feel like it was skipping beats. My upper lip, my hands, and under arms would begin to perspire. If I walked too far away from my house, I would begin to panic turning back immediately. I feared someone was going to put poison in a can of green beans or in my Coke can. Things got so bad that I would awaken in the night in sheer terror. Getting up, I would walk the floors, wringing my hands and moaning.*

*"I had just come out of a season of deep depression when my wife invited me to attend a 'revival' meeting in our church with her. During that meeting I became aware that I*

*was lost and undone without Jesus. I deeply repented of my ways, receiving Jesus as my Lord.*

*"As an after thought, I believed that this decision might help the panic situation. For a while it seemed better, but it would come back with a vengeance. Four months later I surrendered to the call to be a vocational pastor. While in seminary I was constantly open to avenues of healing, but none came.*

*"For the next few years I would drink warm milk at night and listen to sweet, Christian, instrumental music while I slept. I went to a church in San Antonio, Texas for deliverance from a spirit of fear only to have even worse episodes. I heard that inner healing would help so I went through extended times of inner healing with gifted people. I would pray in the Spirit, which would help for a while. I broke inner vows, broke generational curses, and relished in new-found truths about my identity in Christ. All the time during this search for freedom, I began feeling better. Even though occasionally I still had a panic attack, faith was growing in me that I was going to be free.*

*"In the beginning of my second pastorate, my wife and I were driving to a meeting in Childress, Texas, when she played a tape for me that was from a radio program called "Point of View." It was of a woman who began describing her healing and deliverance from the same thing I had experienced for years. I immediately made an appointment with her and she explained that the trigger to her problem had been stress-related. Since she had the same exact symptoms that I had, I decided that I could be free too. I thought I was the only person in the world who had what I had. I had hoped the doctors would have an answer because in my thinking it would have been easier to deal with.*

*"One morning in 1981, while I was on a fast and in a quiet*

*time with the Lord, I 'happened' to find a passage of Scripture in Nehemiah. Nehemiah was on a fast when he prayed and confessed the sins of the children of Israel against the Lord. He also confessed his sins and the sins of his father's house (Neh 1:6). It seemed to me that he so identified with his family that as a representative of his family he cried out for forgiveness. It is not possible that individual sins of family members be forgiven by my confession for that was their responsibility. I am convinced, however, that God not only sees individuals, but also family units.*

*"The moment I stood before the Lord representing my ancestors, sins began to stream through my mind. I repented on behalf of my family what God was seeing from the beginning. Immediately the Spirit spoke, telling me to command the spirit of fear to leave me. I did and IT WAS GONE. I believe that I learned many things during the ten-year spiritual search for freedom. I feel that each thing I learned was important because each thing took away ground that the enemy had in my life. It culminated that day in complete freedom. I have never had another panic attack and by God's word, never will again. All the glory goes to the Father, the Father of our Lord Jesus Christ and His Spirit."*

## Prayer

*Heavenly Father, help me to learn how to cope with anxiety and panic in a godly way. Teach me how to experience Your peace more fully than I ever have. Thank You that you promised that I am more than a conqueror through Him who loves me, in Jesus' mighty name, Amen.*

# 13

---

# Fear of Failure

*For a righteous [man] may fall seven times and rise again...*

(Proverbs 24:16a)

A ll of us experience failure especially if we attempt anything worthwhile. When God began to show me some truths regarding physical healing it changed the way I prayed in private. As a pastor, however, my public prayers for healings lacked power and, consequently, produced few results. When people asked me to pray for them I couched my words in innocuous terminology such as, "If it be Your will," or "Lord, give them peace as they face this trial," or "God, guide the hands of the doctors." There is nothing wrong with the last two requests but how much better it is to boldly pray expecting a miracle.

God wants His children to bring their requests before Him with boldness. Boldness functions as an opposite of fear. The Word of the Lord states it plainly: *The wicked flee when no one pursues, but the righteous are bold as a lion* (Proverbs 28:1).

To be transparent, one reason I hesitated to boldly pray for healing in a public forum is because I was afraid of failure. "What if they don't get healed? Everyone will know my prayer wasn't effective and I'm not such a great prayer warrior after all." I believe other pastors in their heart of hearts feel the same way. We're afraid of failure. Can you see how selfish that kind of fear can be?

The problem is the fear of failure leads to failure. That is because when we have the fear of failure we either refuse to get started or we approach everything with a negative, self-defeating attitude. When we are afraid to get started or do everything with a negative attitude we shoot ourselves in the foot. We almost guarantee the very failure we are trying so hard to avoid. The fear of failure leads to cowardice, inaction and negative decision-making—the recipe for defeat.[xxi]

Failure is not that bad. God doesn't love me any less when I fail. Nothing can separate me from His love, not even my mistakes. It's not so hard to risk when I know my Father loves me unconditionally. I don't see 100% of the people I pray for get healed, but I do see far more people healed today than I used to.

The apostle Peter has been criticized for failing to continue to walk on the water (see Matthew 14:22-33). Personally, I admire Peter because he was willing to get out of the boat. That's a lot more than we can say about the other disciples who remained in the relative safety of the boat.

If a major league baseball player succeeds with his bat only 30% of the time at the plate he's a good hitter. However, if he focuses on the times he failed to get a hit he is doomed to achieving a lower batting average. All baseball players experience failure. It is not a question of failing; it's a question of how he responds to failure. The next time he steps up to the plate he must do it with confidence.

Beloved, let me urge you to be bold as a lion as you face new challenges. Don't let fear keep you from stepping out. The fear of failure will make it appear like laziness to those around you because you avoid taking initiative. God ties laziness or slothfulness with fear in Proverbs 22:13: *The lazy man says, "There is a lion outside! I shall be slain in the streets."* It's not that you are a slacker; it's that you're afraid to get going on a project for fear of failure.

Once you succumb to the fear of failure then your failures increase due to inertia. Then comes shame, lack of confidence, self-deprecation, etc., and the problems snowball. Failure isn't so bad if you don't let it in your heart.

Did you know that the Bible connects fear with shame? David said, *I sought the LORD, and he heard me, and delivered me from all my **fears**. They looked unto him, and were lightened: and their faces were not **ashamed*** (Psalm 34:4-5, emphases mine). Shame says, "I am a failure," rather than "I blew that one," or "I made a mistake." People who go into shame think they are worthless, stupid, incapable of success or unlovable. Toxic shame never comes from God, and God never shames us in this way. He convicts us but doesn't shame us.

Now is the time to act and rid your life of this debilitating fear of failure. Go after it like you would a snake that crawled into your home. I guarantee you that you won't just learn to live with that snake but you will do everything possible to expel it.

Teddy Roosevelt made one of the most powerful statements on the subject I have ever read.

*"It is not the critic who counts, not the man who points out how the strong man stumbled, or where the doers of deeds could have done them better. The credit belongs to the man who is actually in the arena; whose face is marred by dust and sweat*

*and blood; who strives valiantly; who errs and comes up short again and again.....who knows the great enthusiasms, the great devotions, and spends himself in a worthy cause; who at best, knows in the end the triumph of high achievement; and who, at worst, if he fails, at least fails while daring greatly, so that his place shall never be with those cold and timid souls who know neither defeat nor victory."*

## Prayer

*Father in Heaven, I confess that I came into agreement with the fear of failure and I repent. I ask You to replace the fear of failure with boldness and confidence. I reject the fear of failure and break any agreement given to this spirit. And now I take authority over the fear of failure, I bind and break your power, cancel your assignments and cast you out, in the name of Jesus.*

# 14

## Fear of Judgement

*(1) Therefore, having been justified by faith, we have peace with God through our Lord Jesus Christ. (18) Therefore, as through one man's offense [judgment] came to all men, resulting in condemnation, even so through one Man's obedience many will be made righteous.*

(Romans 5:1, 18)

As I minister to people many reveal to me that they live in fear that God will judge them. They worry that they will not measure up or fail in some way and God will punish them. Keep in mind that there is a healthy fear of the Lord mentioned throughout scripture, but that is vastly different from fearing God's judgment.

When Jesus died on the cross, God placed all of His wrath for our sins upon His Son. When I appropriate by faith what Jesus did for me on Calvary, God declares that I am justified. Justification means that I have been acquitted of guilt and have been pronounced righteous. God wipes away all enmity between Him and me and peace is declared.

The peace the apostle Paul mentions in the above verse speaks of the reconciliation that took place between God and all who believe in Him. It does not refer to an inner peace of mind, but will lead to it. The word "peace" was written in the present tense in the original language, meaning that it is an ongoing reality. In other words, the war is over and we are at peace with God.

World War II did not neatly end with Japan's surrender on September 2, 1945. At its height the Japanese Empire was more than 20 million square miles of land and sea. Legend has it that soldiers in isolated regions fought on for years after the surrender. Some were unaware the war had ended; others refused to believe. Some hid in the jungles alone; others fought in groups and continued to make attacks and conduct guerilla warfare. These men were called Japanese Holdouts, or Stragglers, and their stories are some of the most fascinating human interest stories of the 20th Century. [xxii]

Tragically, in the same way, many Christians don't know the war has ended. I feel sorry for the believers who don't realize that the enmity between them and God ceased at the cross. God signed the peace treaty with the blood of His own Son.

The good news is that God no longer holds judgment over our heads because of our sin: *Jesus became sin for us that we might be made the righteousness of God in Him* (2 Corinthians 5:21). If you by faith have received Jesus Christ as your personal Lord and Savior there is now not one single thing you can do to make God love you more. And there is nothing you can do to make Him love you any less. If you mess up, God is not mad at you—He is not out to get you and make your life miserable. He won't send sickness, disease, poverty, and loss of relationships. If you sin He's not going to bring tragedy in your life and send you to hell. He doesn't condemn you.

You say, "Roger, don't you believe in holy living?" Absolutely! I strongly advocate holy living, but not to get God to love me or accept me or withhold His judgment. We are already accepted when we are in Christ (Ephesians 1:4-6). I will admit, however, that if you have no desire to live a pure life before God you are telling me that you don't really know the Lord and haven't been genuinely saved. When He comes into our hearts He changes our desires.

You might be saying to yourself, "If you teach this doctrine of free grace people will go out and live in sin." If you had that response that is good! It means you are really thinking seriously about justification. Evidently Paul got the same reaction after teaching about justification by faith so he had to bring these truths into balance: *What then? Shall we sin because we are not under law but under grace? Certainly not* (Romans 6:15)!

It is foolish to willfully sin and here are a few reasons why. First, sin harms us and the people around us. Sometimes there are even health ramifications. For example, bitterness may open the door to arthritis or other illnesses. Second, sin gives the devil an inroad into our lives (Ephesians 4:26-27). Third, it is a poor witness and a bad example to those we influence. Fourth, it is contrary to our new nature in Christ. And fifth, willful sin can create a dullness of heart so that it becomes difficult to hear God's voice. Yet, God doesn't judge me or hate me when I sin because all the fury of His wrath was placed on Jesus on the cross. When I understand the truth that God loves me unconditionally it makes me want to love Him in return and turn away from any willful sin. Scripture clearly says that the goodness of God leads us to repentance (Romans 2:4).

You might protest, "You mean to say that all my striving to do good doesn't count?" No, not in respect to gaining God's approval. What we do through the power of the Spirit will be rewarded both in this life and in the life to come. However, nothing you accomplish for Jesus in the strength of your flesh will last. Only what Christ is able to do through you will reap eternal rewards. What we accomplish in the power of our own ability is like wood, hay, and straw and will be burned up: *Each one's work will become clear; for the Day will declare it, because it will be revealed by fire; and the fire will test each one's work, of what sort it is. If anyone's work is burned, he will suffer loss; but he himself will be saved, yet so as through fire* (1 Corinthians 3:15).

Beloved, please know that God is not out to judge you for your shortcomings. He is not looking for a way to zap you and make your life miserable. He loves you and yearns for fellowship with you and delights in you. If you sin He will bring discipline, not because He's mad at you, but because He has your welfare in mind and desires to correct your course. The primary way He disciplines His children is through the Word: *All Scripture is given by inspiration of God, and is profitable for doctrine, for reproof, for correction, in righteousness* (2 Timothy 3:16). He also uses such things as circumstances, the words of other Christians, and dreams. But never forget that if He corrects you it is because He loves you.

## Prayer

*Father in heaven, I thank You and praise You for what You did for me on the cross. Thank You that You have declared me righteous. Sometimes I don't feel very righteous but I base my life on Your Word rather than my feelings. I reject and renounce the religious spirit that would tell me that I have to work to earn Your acceptance and approval. I choose to rest in Your finished work and I open up my heart to receive Your loving embrace. And now I command the fear of judgment to leave me and go to dry places, in the name of Jesus, Amen.*

# 15

---

# Fear of Lack or Poverty

*"Therefore I say to you, do not worry about your life, what you will eat or what you will drink; nor about your body, what you will put on. Is not life more than food and the body more than clothing? Look at the birds of the air, for they neither sow nor reap nor gather into barns; yet your heavenly Father feeds them. Are you not of more value than they? Which of you by worrying can add one cubit to his stature? So why do you worry about clothing? Consider the lilies of the field, how they grow: they neither toil nor spin; and yet I say to you that even Solomon in all his glory was not arrayed like one of these. Now if God so clothes the grass of the field, which today is, and tomorrow is thrown into the oven, will He not much more clothe you, O you of little faith? Therefore do not worry, saying, `What shall we eat?' or `What shall we drink?' or `What shall we wear?' For it is the Gentiles who strive for all these things; and indeed your heavenly Father knows that you need all these things."*

(Matthew 6:25-32)

In 1933, construction of the famous Golden Gate Bridge began. The projected price tag was a whopping thirty-five million. Imagine what it would cost in today's dollars! In those days, the anticipated fatality rate was one person for every million spent. The expected thirty-five deaths proved unacceptable to bridge-builder Joseph Strauss. Consequently, he took every precaution imaginable to keep his workers safe. One of these precautions was the installation of a safety net, previously unheard of in the business of bridge construction. The cost of the net—a hefty one hundred and twenty-five thousand dollars. However, Strauss believed that he could easily recoup the expense because the workers would work faster without the fear that they would die if they fell. Although they worked in dangerous conditions, suspended 220 feet above the water battling high winds, the men felt safe knowing that the net was there. As it turned out, the net proved itself a worthwhile investment, having saved the lives of nineteen grateful men.[xxiii]

We function better when we feel secure. Unfortunately, we often try to find security in something or someone other than God. Some people think they will be secure if only they have enough money. So they lay up money in bank accounts, stocks, and other tangible assets. But money cannot protect us from heartbreak, failure, sin, disease, or disaster in this world.

Other people think they will be secure because of their training, skills, or talents. But even the best educated are not immune to sudden reversals of fortune. Still others expect security from their families, friends, or business connections. But these are only human supports. The truth is the security of this world is nothing but an illusion. The only true security comes from God Himself. God should be our safety net.

Jesus promised that if we'd seek first His Kingdom then God would supply all of "these things" (Matthew 6:33). When Jesus died for us on the cross He took care of all our basic needs. The apostle Paul put it this way: *For you know the grace of our Lord Jesus Christ, that though He was rich, yet for your sakes He became poor, that you through His poverty might become rich* (2 Corinthians 8:9). Some people try to spiritualize this verse but the context plainly shows he's talking about material goods. I'm not saying that if you put Christ first in your life that you're going to have two Rolls Royces and three Mercedes in your 5,000-square-foot garage. But the Bible promises that you have already been provided for by your heavenly Father.

I heard about a man who took an ocean voyage years ago and he didn't have much money. He was trying to get from the old country to the new country so he packed his lunch, which consisted of hard biscuits, cheese, and tea. Day after day he ate this in his room. Finally he got sick of the same old thing. He was walking past the dining area and he smelled the delicious food. Finally he broke down. He did have a little money and he asked the steward, "How much would it cost to eat in there?" The steward inquired, "Sir, do you have a ticket?" He replied, "Yes." The steward remarked, "Well don't you know that when you bought a ticket for your voyage that that included all of your meals? Don't you know that?" I feel sorry for people who are on their way to heaven second-class when they could be feasting on the riches of all that God has provided.

One of my favorite promises in the Bible involves God's provision. *And my God shall supply all your need according to His riches in glory by Christ Jesus* (Philippians 4:19). When we consider the context of this verse we realize he is saying that if we give generously to Kingdom purposes then God will supply our needs. All the promises of God regarding our material well-being carry a condition.

God's Word is full of promises regarding our material provision. It will help build your faith by becoming familiar with these verses.

*I have been young, and now am old; yet I have not seen the righteous forsaken, nor his descendants begging bread* (Psalm 37:25).

*Let the LORD be magnified, Who has pleasure in the prosperity of His servant* (Psalm 35:27b).

*The young lions do lack and suffer hunger; but those who seek the LORD shall not lack any good thing* (Psalm 34:10).

*The generous soul will be made rich, and he who waters will also be watered himself* (Proverbs 11:25).

*He who trusts in his riches will fall, but the righteous will flourish like foliage* (Proverbs 11:28).

*"And the LORD will make you the head and not the tail; you shall be above only, and not be beneath, if you heed the commandments of the LORD your God, which I command you today, and are careful to observe them"* (Deuteronomy 28:13).

*"This Book of the Law shall not depart from your mouth, but you shall meditate in it day and night, that you may observe to do according to all that is written in it. For then you will make your way prosperous, and then you will have good success"* (Joshua 1:8).

*But this I say: He who sows sparingly will also reap sparingly, and he who sows bountifully will also reap bountifully. So let each one [give] as he purposes in his heart, not grudgingly or of necessity; for God loves a cheerful giver. And God is able to make all grace abound toward you, that you, always having all sufficiency in all things, may have an abundance for every good work* (2 Corinthians 9:6-8).

God promises to provide our needs. Since He is our source we don't need to fear poverty. Our security rests in His very Name, Jehovah-Jireh (our source, sufficiency, and provider). Money alone does not satisfy the need for security. Six highly paid executives were interviewed by a news person. The question was asked, "What is your greatest fear?" Each answered much the same, using different words. Their greatest fear was that they would not have enough money. When they were asked, "How much is enough?" they always answered, "A little more." It seems the world's goods never completely satisfy.<sup>xxiv</sup>

## Prayer

*Father in heaven, I thank You that in Christ You have already provided my needs. Help me fulfill the conditions of Your promises<sup>xxv</sup> so I can receive what is already mine. Please forgive me for trusting in material wealth. My only true security is in You and I declare that You are my provider. Fear of poverty and fear of lack, I reject and renounce you and I command you to leave me now, in Jesus' name, Amen.*

# 16

---

# Fear of Natural Disasters

*Therefore we will not fear, even though the earth be removed, and though the mountains be carried into the midst of the sea; though its waters roar and be troubled, though the mountains shake with its swelling. Selah.*

(Psalm 46:2-3)

arry Hinshaw, living in Southern California, said that for days after an earthquake when there were little tremors, their children would run terrified and screaming into their bedroom thinking it was happening again. He said that on that morning they couldn't get into Debbie and Carol's bedroom because both beds had jammed against the door. Larry said that he called out through the doors, "Be calm. Don't worry, we Hinshaws are noted for our cool heads in the face of emergencies." Inside he heard a frail little voice which sobbed out, "Daddy, I think we take after mama's side of the family." xxvi

Sometimes people's reactions to earthquakes are humorous. Ruthie and I thought it was funny after moving to Texas from

California when we heard people's remarks. When Texans found out what region we came from they would often ask, "California? How could you stand living in California with all those earthquakes?" Our come back was, "How can you stand living here with all these tornados?" The truth is, we did not live in fear because of the threat of another earthquake when we lived in the San Francisco Bay Area because we got used to the ground periodically shaking and rolling. Wherever you live, whether it is in Florida with its massive hurricanes, Washington State with its volcanic activity, Texas with its hailstorms, or Southern California with its devastating wildfires, there is always an opportunity for fear to take over if we allow it.

In recent years another natural disaster fear has surfaced—the fear of a massive asteroid striking the earth. I've read some articles and pamphlets recalling past asteroid contact with the earth and some assert that one such collision resulted in the Ice Age. *USA Today* (February 23, 2001) stated that a comet might have triggered mass extinction, including all the dinosaurs. Some reason that, since large meteorites have historically struck the earth every so many years, we are due for another one.[xxvii]

According to an article in the *Times Union* (July 1, 1991), "Scientists gathered together today to find how or to make plans how to divert killer asteroids." (That sounds like a Hollywood movie.) CNN reported on July 24, 2002 that astronomers are carefully monitoring a 1.2-mile wide asteroid that is on a collision course with our planet. Calculations indicate that it will hit the earth on February 1, 2019 and if it does it will cause incredible damage. *Reuter's News* stated that a disaster this size would create a worldwide meltdown of our economy and social life. It would reduce all nations to Dark Age conditions.[xxviii]

The Southern Asian and East African countries continue to deal with the aftermath of a monster tsunami. The death count climbed to around 150,000 and 5 million suffered loss. A large percentage of children died and the reason some give is because they innocently went to the beach to play in the extraordinarily large waves. They did not know that these waves were the precursor to an approaching massive 50 foot wall of water.

Hurricane Katrina left tens of thousands homeless as much of New Orleans was buried under 20 feet of water. Sadly, many people in Louisiana lost everything they owned because of this category 4 storm.

Yes, it is understandable that a person could be gripped by the fear of natural disasters. What can we do? There are some practical actions which wisdom would direct, such as doing common sense things to avoid danger. For example, don't build your house so close to the beach. If you live in Southern California with its wild fires, make sure you build an adequate firebreak around your home and use tile roofing instead of shake or composite. There are many safety procedures that should be followed, but no matter what precautions we take we are never completely free of the threat of tragedy.

The key to victory entails embracing an eternal perspective. Remember, there is no real security apart from God. All natural security is nothing but an illusion, for nothing on this planet is entirely safe. Notice what the psalmist went on to say: *There is a river whose streams shall make glad the city of God, the holy place of the tabernacle of the Most High* (Psalm 46:11).

These words refer to two realities. The first reference is to the earthly city of Jerusalem, located in ancient Palestine. The backdrop of the psalm was most likely some great intervention of God to defeat the enemy armies that had come against Israel. In this time of insecurity and upheaval those who lived within the walls of Jerusalem were safe. With this in mind, the "river" of verse 4 refers to the stream of Siloam, the natural supply of fresh water in Jerusalem. The residents didn't have to worry about their drinking water supply being cut off by a siege against the city. The "holy place" points to the temple mount and thus, the

Presence of God.

The second reference is to the spiritual Jerusalem, a symbol of heaven, which is being prepared by God for His elect children. Think about it! Believers are destined for a Kingdom that cannot be shaken. In the heavenly Jerusalem frame of reference the "river" of verse 4 is the river that flows from God's throne (See Revelation 22:1-2), and the "holy place" is the third heaven or the dwelling place of God. In Hebrews 11:10 we learn that Abraham looked not for a mere earthly Jerusalem but the city "whose builder and maker is God." Martin Luther, the great reformer, based his famous hymn, *A Mighty Fortress Is Our God* on the Psalm 46. He knew that God is unshakable and trustworthy. Here are some of the words to his hymn:

> Let goods and kindred go,
> This mortal life also;
> The body they may kill:
> God's truth abideth still;
> His kingdom is forever.

The reality is that God alone is the source of true security. He is the one who holds the whole universe together by the Word of His power. Therefore, He is the only one who I should run to for safety. Let these words sink into your heart: *Be still, and know that I am God; I will be exalted among nations, I will be exalted in the earth* (Psalm 46:10)!

# Prayer

*Heavenly Father, I repent for having come into agreement with the fear of natural disasters. This sin is wicked, ungodly, and against You. I receive Your forgiveness and the blood of Jesus Christ cleanses me now. I renounce this fear in my life and in my generations past on both sides of my family. You evil spirit of fear, it is written, "If the son, therefore, shall make you free, ye shall be free indeed." I cancel any commitment, break any contract and take back any territory given you through this sin of coming into agreement with you. I command you to leave me now and go to dry places! I close this door to your activity in my life, in Jesus' name. Thank You Heavenly Father for the freedom You have given me, in Jesus' mighty name, Amen.*

# 17

---

# Fear of Persecution

*But even if you should suffer for righteousness, sake, you
are blessed. "And do not be afraid of their threats, nor be
troubled."*

(1 Peter 3:14)

**P**ersecution hurts especially when it comes from family
members or trusted friends. Whenever you make a stand for
Christ and go against the flow of popular opinion expect a certain
level of persecution. Generally in America we don't suffer to
the same extent that many believers do throughout the world.
Nevertheless, negative words and ostracism still hurt deeply.
Because of the potential pain, it's easy for the enemy to sow the
seeds of fear of persecution into our hearts.

If anyone knew anything about persecution it was the Christians
to whom the apostle Peter wrote. In his first epistle he teaches
us how to respond when we get attacked due to our spiritual
convictions. Peter delineates at least three reactions to avoid
when faced with mistreatment.

First, **don't be astonished**. *Beloved, do not think it strange concerning the fiery trial which is to try you, as though some strange thing happened to you* (1 Peter 4:12). Like the Christians of the first century many believers today have false expectations. They think, "If I live right, do right, and think right, God's favor will rest upon me and therefore, people will treat me right." So it surprises them when they suffer mistreatment. It catches them off guard. The basis of the surprise is that in their heart of hearts they believe persecution is not supposed to happen.

Let's realign our expectations with the Word of God. In the Sermon on the Mount Jesus describes the person who is a member of the Kingdom of God. He is poor in spirit, and gentle, and he hungers for righteousness (Matthew 5:3-10). And then notice the last Beatitude and the verses following: *"Blessed are those who are persecuted for righteousness' sake, for theirs is the kingdom of heaven. Blessed are you when they revile and persecute you, and say all kinds of evil against you falsely for My sake. Rejoice and be exceedingly glad, for great is your reward in heaven, for so they persecuted the prophets who were before you"* (Matthew 5:10-12). Jesus is saying that when you live up to the first seven beatitudes the world is going to respond with persecution.

Jesus lived a perfect life and love exuded from his very being. Yet His character drew out the hatred and the envy of the world. Jesus tried to help His disciples develop realistic expectations and prepare them to suffer for His name: *"Remember the word that I said to you, 'A servant is not greater than his master.' If they persecuted Me, they will also persecute you. If they kept My word, they will keep yours also"* (John 15:20). If this reaction is what dedicated Christians should expect, then the truth is, we should be surprised if we don't suffer persecution.

Second, **don't be angry**. *For this is commendable, if because of conscience toward God one endures grief, suffering wrongfully. For what credit is it if, when you are beaten for your faults, you* *take it patiently? But when you do good and suffer, if you take it patiently, this is commendable before God. For to this you were called, because Christ also suffered for us, leaving us an example, that you should follow His steps: "Who committed no sin, Nor was deceit found in His mouth": who, when He was reviled, did not revile in return: when He suffered, He did not threaten, but committed Himself to Him who judges righteously* (1 Peter 2:19-23). The amazing characteristic of Jesus was the fact that when He was mistreated He did not get mad and retaliate. On the cross He cried out, *"Father, forgive them, for they do not know what they do..."* (Luke 23:34).

The third reaction to avoid is fear. **Don't be afraid.** *And who is he that will harm you if you become followers of what is good? But even if you should suffer for righteousness' sake, you are blessed. "And do not be afraid of their threats, nor be troubled"* (1 Peter 3:13-14). Don't get intimidated by their caustic words or threats. The word "troubled" means "agitated" or "stirred up." You might be thinking, "You mean to say that when people reject, slander, and falsely accuse me, I'm not to be distressed?"

That's right! The reason for our peace is found in these verses. No one can really harm us if we are truly following Jesus. You say, "It sure feels like harm to me." Keep in mind that we're not talking about harm to our external shell. No, the only real harm comes when we allow the pain to get into our heart. A person can suffer on the outside and not suffer harm on the inside. No one can wound the inner life unless we give them permission.

In fact, persecution has a purifying effect on our human spirit if we will let it. In 1991 I accepted a senior pastoral role in a church in California. Though we witnessed many conversions and baptisms many people reacted negatively to my strong messages regarding the Lordship of Jesus Christ. Consequently, a significant number of the established leadership left, taking with them a high percentage of our budgetary needs.

The decrease in the budget and leadership pool made it impossible to continue with the same quality programs. As discontentment began to brew, the atmosphere became tense and people started to question my leadership ability. I was determined to hang in there and to pour my heart and soul into turning things around.

Then one day the deacons called a special business meeting for the purpose of voting me out of the church. The congregation decided to let me go thinking that was best in light of the situation. When I got the news of their decision it devastated me. It felt like someone had kicked me in the stomach and ripped my guts out.

I went outside and sat on my patio and began to pray and weep. With tears I cried out, "Why God? I worked so hard and I only tried to do my best. Why did this happen? I thought you called me to this church." Then I had an amazing experience. I fell into a trance-like state and experienced a vision. In the vision I saw a big flip chart, sort of like a large Rolodex file. Only instead of having names and addresses on each card there were pictures depicting sins and bad habits God had taken from my life.

The scenes were displayed in chronological order beginning from the day of my conversion experience to the present. The pages flipped over one at a time. As I viewed the pictures one by one I rejoiced that God had indeed done a great work in my life to make me more like Jesus. Then the flip chart came to the last one. Instead of a picture there was one word printed in big black bold letters—**SELF.**

I asked, "Lord, what does this mean?" The Lord said, "I have delivered you of a lot of junk over the years. Now I am working on self and that's the hardest one to deal with." The light went on and I could see what God was doing and I replied, "Lord, if that's what You're doing in the midst of this horrible situation then by all means deal with my self-life." My heart filled with hope as I saw that God was using the crisis to purify my character.

Think how the patriarch Joseph felt when his own brothers sold him into slavery. While serving in Potiphar's house he suffered false accusation and was subsequently sent to prison. Later, after he was used to save his family, he told his brothers about God's greater plan: *"But as for you, you meant evil against me; but God meant it for good, in order to bring it about as it is this day, to save many people alive"* (Genesis 50:20).

Beloved, why do we fear persecution? It's because we don't see things from God's perspective. God uses mistreatment to bring us to a higher level and to further His Kingdom. He desires to strip us of all selfish ambition and pride and to demonstrate how He can cause good to come out of evil.

## Prayer

*Father in heaven, please forgive me for being short-sighted and not seeing things from an eternal perspective. I repent for the times I did not speak boldly about You for fear of persecution. I reject and renounce the fear of persecution and I command this fear to leave me now and go to dry places, in the name of Jesus, Amen.*

# 18

---

# Fear of Public Speaking

*The fear of man brings a snare, but whoever trusts in the
LORD shall be safe.*

(Proverbs 29:25)

"Kevin, I got a note from your high school teacher, saying
you've been missing your history class," his mother
inquired? In the tenth grade his teacher required that the students
make a presentation in front of the class. Rather than give the
speech Kevin chose to skip class knowing that he would have
to face the consequences. "I don't like my teacher; I think he's
a communist," Kevin lied, trying to touch a sensitive nerve with
his staunch anti-communist mother. His mind went numb with
disbelief as she actually bought his story.

Something happened in his heart that school year that affected
him for years. When he ran from the fear of public speaking
it only intensified. He did everything his creative mind could
conjure up to avoid getting up in front of a group of people.

Imagine the struggle he went through at age 21 when God called him to preach. He vividly recalls his first sermon. His church led a service once a month at a rescue mission on skid row in San Francisco. The men's group asked him to preach, so he agreed, thinking that it would not be too bad standing in front of a group of inebriated homeless men.

After they sang a few hymns, Kevin's turn came to approach the platform. He stood behind the pulpit with his knees shaking so violently he wondered if he could continue to remain upright. His mouth got so dry, his tongue stuck to the roof of his mouth and he barely got the words out. About half way through the sermon, a man in the audience passed out and hit his head with a loud thud on the back of the pew in front of him. Everyone's attention focused on the poor unconscious gentleman, as he required first aid treatment.

That was Kevin's great debut to a career of preaching the gospel of Christ. It didn't get much easier for a long time. What helped him was to focus on his love for people rather than on himself. But Kevin says the thing that helped him the most was simply facing the fear. The more he preached the easier it became. Eventually he got to the place where he actually enjoyed getting up in front of a congregation.

The principle I have learned is this: You overcome your fears by walking through them. When you run from your fears they only intensify. I believe God orchestrates situations to give us opportunities to face our fears. As we walk through the fear we get to the place where we no longer fear it.

Studies indicate that the fear of public speaking ranks as the number one fear for the average American. Most people don't mind speaking in front of small groups of friends but they seek to avoid center stage at large gatherings. Granted, God has not gifted everyone with oratory talent, nor has He called everyone to a ministry of public speaking. But when we give in to fear and run from it we empower the enemy. If he gains ground in one area of fear it will be easier for him to set up other areas and keep the strongman of fear in place. The scripture says, "The fear of man brings a snare" (The fear of public speaking is a form of the fear of man.) In Biblical times a hunter used a snare to catch his prey and Satan will use this fear to ensnare you.

When God called Moses to lead the Children of Israel out of Egypt, Moses answered the LORD, *"O my Lord, I am not eloquent, neither before nor since You have spoken to Your servant; but I am slow of speech and of a slow tongue."* Then the Lord reassured him by asking, *"Who has made man's mouth? O who makes the mute, the deaf, the seeing, or the blind? Have not I, the LORD?"* Then God went on to say, *"Now therefore go, and I will be with your mouth, and teach you what you shall say"* (Exodus 4:10-12).

Did Moses trust God and take Him at His word? No. He chose to run saying, "Send someone else." Then the anger of the Lord was kindled against Moses. But God, in His mercy, agreed to let Aaron his brother be the spokesman. God used Aaron but it would have been better if Moses had simply trusted the Lord.

If God leads you to speak in front of a large group just do it. As He promised Moses, He will be with your mouth. Put more faith in God's word than you place in your fears. The more you do it the easier it becomes.

When I was preparing the first message to preach in my home church my mother sensed my nervousness and gave me wise advice. She said, "Keep your eyes off yourself and on the needs of the people." How true and helpful those words have been. The Lord Himself said, *There is no fear in love; but perfect love casts out fear* (1 John 4:18a).

While in college a classmate told me his secret to overcoming his fear of public speaking. He said, "When I get up there in front of everyone I look out on the audience and imagine that they all have goat heads." I've never taken his advice but I think I know what he was trying to say. Don't take yourself too seriously. Just relax and have fun with the people and let God be with your mouth.

## Prayer

*Father in heaven, I confess that the fear of man is sin. I repent for any time I have yielded to the fear of public speaking and I renounce it as sin. I ask that I would be more conscious of the needs of the people I speak to than I am of what they think of me. By Your grace I will not run away from the opportunities when You lead me to speak in public. I ask for boldness, in Jesus' name, Amen.*

# 19

---

# Fear versus Love

*There is no fear in love; but perfect love casts out fear,*
*because fear involves torment. But he who fears has not*
*been made perfect in love.*

(1 John 4:18)

Another opposite of fear is love because, as the above verse
says, perfect love casts out fear. This realization offers
another key in defeating fear. If love casts out fear then it stands
to reason that we should get filled up with love, especially the
love of God because His love is perfect. God loves you and His
love is unconditional.

I was raised in a Christian home where we went to church
every Sunday. I was baptized at age nine mainly because it was
something my friends did. However, when I entered my teenage
years I became quite rebellious. I rebelled against my parents
and I rebelled against God. My parents forced me to go to church

against my will so in anger I made an inner vow that I would never step foot inside a church again once I became of age. I hated it when someone would try to preach to me or invite me to church. I avoided anything that remotely sounded like "church music."

After years of rebellion and alcohol and drug abuse my life was in shambles. Late one night, in alcoholic DT's and desperation I cried out to God, "Lord, I want to be a Christian now." I was expecting bells and whistles but I felt absolutely nothing. So I cried out again, "Lord, I want to be a Christian!" Still nothing. It felt like my prayer was getting no higher than the ceiling.

Again I prayed with the same response. Finally the thought occurred to me, "Roger, you have known the truth for a long time and you have rejected Jesus to the extent that now you have passed the point of no return and you cannot be saved no matter what you do." This thought terrified me. I broke out into a cold sweat and in tears I begged God to save me. I prayed this way for what seemed like hours.

Finally, the Lord spoke to me so clearly it seemed like an audible voice. "Roger, you are just trying to use Me to get you through this rough time in your life. After things smooth out you're going to go back to living your life for yourself. If you really want Me to save you, you must make Jesus the Lord of your life." As desperate as I was I had to think about that statement. As I reasoned in my mind I came to the conclusion that if Jesus created me and He died to save me from my sins, then He had the right to be my Lord.

So I said, "Jesus, I want You to be the Lord and Savior of my life." The moment I said those words, wow! Something happened and I was immediately changed. I felt a heavy load had been lifted off my shoulders and I was clean on the inside. Everything became new to me and I saw life in a totally different light. I was born again!

I couldn't get enough of the Bible–I read it for literally hours every day. Several days after my experience I was reading in the Gospel of John where Jesus said, *"Ye have not chosen me, but I have chosen you..."* (John 15:16). The words hit me between the eyes. As the realization sunk in, joy flooded my heart because, based on my experience, I thought God saved me because I coerced Him with all my begging and pleading to save me. But through that verse God showed me that before I prayed that prayer that night, He had already been reaching out to me to draw me to Himself.

The truth is there is not one thing you can do to get God to love you or to earn His acceptance. Conversely, there is not one single thing you can do to make God not love you or reject you. If you mess up, God is not mad at you. He's not out to make your life miserable. He's not going to bring tragedy into your life to teach you a lesson, and He's not condemning you for your mistakes.

The only way anyone can get right with God is through faith in Jesus Christ. The whole issue concerns righteousness. In our day the big question is, "If God is a loving God, how can He send anyone to hell?" But the right question is, "How can a holy God send an unholy people to a perfect heaven and still maintain His integrity?"

God's solution to the problem was He loved us so much He sent His Son to die for us. All of the sin of humanity was placed upon Jesus when He hung on the cross. He identified with our sin to the extent that scripture says He actually became sin. Paul put it this way: *For He made Him who knew no sin to be sin for us, that we might become the righteousness of God in Him* (2 Corinthians 5:21).

One time I attended a conference led by Peter Lord. He asked the audience this question: "Who is more righteous, Jesus or you?" The immediate response was, "Jesus, of course." But Peter Lord challenged us to think again. If God made me righteous and

Jesus lives in me, then when God looks at me He sees the very righteousness of His Son. The correct answer is that Jesus and I share the same righteousness.

Along these lines let me ask another question: "Who does the Father love more—Jesus or you?" Again the correct answer is that He loves you both the same. Think about that measure of love. When I meditate on the greatness of His love it takes my breath away!

The religious leaders during Jesus' day taught that one must strive to keep all of the Old Testament laws. However, the New Testament teaches that no one is saved by keeping the law. In fact the law was given to show us how desperately we need the Savior. The good news is that when I placed my faith in Christ as my personal Lord and Savior, God the Father declared that I was made righteous as a gift and not as a result of my good works.

Paul boldly stated, *For by grace are ye saved by faith; and that not of yourselves: it is the gift of God: Not of works, lest any man should boast* (Ephesians 2:8-9). Our works don't get us to heaven. They follow us to heaven but they don't get us there. The reason I obey the Lord is because I love Him. I love Him because He first loved me.

At this point someone might complain, "If you tell people that God loves them, no matter what, they're just going to go out and live in sin!" I disagree with this objection because the Bible clearly says, *The goodness of God leads you to repentance* (Romans 2:4b).

Please don't misunderstand me. I'm all for holy living and I highly encourage it. But we don't live holy lives to get God to love or accept us. There are many reasons to keep our lives pure. First, it's not our nature now, as born again believers, to live a lifestyle of sin. Second, sin is harmful to us and people around us. It robs us of our joy and peace and brings untold misery. Third, willful sin gives the devil an inroad and fourth, sinful behavior is a bad example and a poor testimony. But we don't live holy lives in order to gain God's love and acceptance. He loves us, warts and all.

When we understand the depth of God's unfailing love, it tends to drive ungodly fear out of our lives. The Lord said to Joshua as he was preparing to lead the Children of Israel into the Promise Land, *"Have I not commanded you? Be strong and of good courage; do not be afraid, nor be dismayed, for the LORD your God is with you wherever you go"* (Joshua 1:9).

Here are some verses to meditate on regarding God's love and acceptance:

*"For the LORD'S portion is his people; Jacob is the place of his inheritance. He found him in a desert land, and in the wasteland, a howling wilderness; He encircled him, He instructed him, He kept him as the apple of his eye"* (Deuteronomy 32:9-10).

*I will praise You, for I am fearfully and wonderfully made; marvelous are Your works, and that my soul knows very well. My frame was not hidden from You, when I was made in secret, And skillfully wrought in the lowest parts of the earth. Your eyes saw my substance, being yet unformed. And in Your book they all were written, the days fashioned for me, when as yet there were none of them. How precious also are Your thoughts to me, O God! How great is the sum of them! If I should count them, they would be more in number than the sand; when I awake, I am still with You* (Psalm 139: 14-18).

*"Can a woman forget her nursing child, and not have compassion on the son of her womb? Surely they may forget, yet I will not forget you. See, I have inscribed you on the palms of my hands; Your walls are continually before Me"* (Isaiah 49:15-16).

*For I know the thoughts that I think toward you, says the LORD, thoughts of peace and not of evil, to give you a future and a hope*

(Jeremiah 29:11).

*"Before I formed you in the womb I knew you; before you were born I sanctified you, I ordained you a prophet to the nations"* (Jeremiah 1:5).

*For thus says the LORD of hosts: "He sent me after glory, to the nations which plunder you; for he who touches you touches the apple of his eye"* (Zechariah 2:8).

*What is man, that You are mindful of him, and the son of man, that You visit him? For You have made him a little lower than the angels, and You have crowned him with glory and honor. You have made him to have dominion over the works of Your hands; You have put all things under his feet* (Psalm 8:4-6).

*"And do not fear those who kill the body but cannot kill the soul. But rather fear Him who is able to destroy both soul and body in hell. Are not two sparrows sold for a copper coin? And not one of them falls to the ground apart from your Father's will. But the very hairs of your head are all numbered. Do not fear therefore; you are of more value than many sparrows"* (Matthew 10:28-31).

*"For God so loved the world, that He gave his only begotten Son, that whoever believes in him should not perish but have everlasting life"* (John 3:16).

*"You did not choose me, but I chose you, and appointed you that you should go and bear fruit, and that your fruit should remain: that whatever you ask of the Father in My name, He may give you"* (John 15:16).

*For you did not receive the spirit of bondage again to fear, but you received the Spirit of adoption by whom we cry out, Abba, Father* (Romans 8:15).

*For He made Him who knew no sin to be sin for us, that we might become the righteousness of God in Him* (2 Corinthians 5:21).

*Therefore you are no more a slave but a son, and if a son, then an heir of God through Christ* (Galatians 4:7).

*For all the law is fulfilled in one word, even in this; "You shall love your neighbor as yourself"* (Galatians 5:14).

*Just as he chose us in Him before the foundation of the world, that we should be holy and without blame before him in love, having predestinated us to the adoption as sons by Jesus Christ to Himself, according to the good pleasure of his will, to the praise of the glory of his grace, by which he made us accepted in the Beloved* (Ephesians 1:4-6).

Hide these scriptures in your heart, open your human spirit to the Father and listen to Him as He speaks His words of love and acceptance over you. Get filled up with the love of God, and one by-product will be that fear will fade away, as you feel the security of His embrace.

## Prayer

*Heavenly Father, I thank You that You loved me before I loved You. Thank You for sending Your Son, Jesus, to die for my sins. Thank You that Your word declares that nothing can separate me from Your love. I open up my heart to You to receive Your love, in Jesus' name, Amen.*

# 20

# Fear versus Faith

*Now if God so clothes the grass of the field, which today is, and tomorrow is thrown into the oven, will he not much more clothe you, O you of little faith?*

(Matthew 6:30)

*Now when he got into a boat, his disciples followed him. And suddenly a great tempest arose on the sea, so that the boat was covered with the waves. But he was asleep. Then His disciples came to him, and awoke Him, saying, "Lord, save us! We are perishing!" But He said to them, "Why are you fearful, O you of little faith?" Then He arose and rebuked the winds and the sea, and there was a great calm.*

(Matthew 8:23-26)

*But when he (Peter) saw that the wind was boisterous, he was afraid; and beginning to sink he cried out, saying, "Lord, save me!" And immediately Jesus stretched out His hand, and caught him, and said to him, "O you of little faith, why did you doubt?"*

(Matthew 14:30-31)

Here are a few instances in scripture that demonstrate the truth that the opposite of faith is fear. When we fear, our faith gets contaminated. Another way to think of it is that our faith becomes neutralized. For example, the way to neutralize an acid is by mixing in a base which acts as an opposite. In the same way, fear is the exact opposite of faith and weakens or neutralizes our ability to believe God.

Keep in mind that the Christian life requires strong faith because the Bible says that without faith it is impossible to please God. Throughout the New Testament miracles happened when people dared to believe God. Jesus said, "According to your faith be it done unto you." He also declared, "If you can believe, all things are possible to him who believes" (Mark 9:23).

In one sense, you cannot not believe. You are always going to believe something. You will either believe God or you will believe Satan. The Word of God states, *Faith comes by hearing, and hearing by the word of God* (Romans 10:17). The reverse way to put it is, "Fear comes by hearing, and hearing by the word of Satan." Don't take fear lightly because any form of fear will give the kingdom of darkness an inroad in that particular area.

I have heard many people seem to brag that they are worry warts, but did you know that when we worry we are actually meditating on fear? Worry is the devil's form of meditation. Worry is fear-based and the tragedy is that most Christians place more faith in what they fear then in what God says in His Word.

Fear is the devil's form of faith, and is a direct opposite to God's faith, just like the South Pole is to the North Pole. While faith is the substance of things hoped for, the evidence of things not seen (Hebrews 11:1), fear is the substance of things not hoped for, the evidence of things not seen. Fear and faith are alike in that they both insist on being fulfilled. Fear is Satan's source of power—faith is God's source of power.[xxix]

A sobering thought is that fear attracts you to the thing you are afraid of. In the same way faith brings things from the spiritual world to the physical world, so fear takes the lies of Satan and causes them to be manifested in our lives.

Scripture teaches that what we fear will come to pass. In Proverbs

10:24 we read, *The fear of the wicked, it shall come upon him.* Job said, *"For the thing which I greatly feared is come upon me, and that which I was afraid of is come unto me"* (Job 3:25). What motivated Job to offer daily sacrifices for his children (Job 1:5)? He was afraid that they might have sinned and cursed God in their hearts.

On the other hand, Scripture teaches that if we believe God, we will get what we need. Let the words of Jesus into your heart: *"If you can believe, all things are possible to him who believes"* (Mark 9:24). He also said, *"Therefore I say to you, whatever things you ask when you pray, believe that you receive them, and you will have them"* (Mark 11:24).

Beloved, don't take fear lightly because in the eyes of God fear is not just weakness; it is wickedness. See what God says about it in the book of Revelation: *But the fearful, and unbelieving, and the abominable, and murderers, and whoremongers, and sorcerers, and idolaters, and all liars, shall have their part in the lake which burneth with fire and brimstone: which is the second death* (Revelation 21:8, KJV). Notice how the Lord groups fear with other horrible sins. See also that fear leads the list of sins. This means that we must confess and repent of fear just like we do any other sin. Beloved, I urge you not to tolerate fear. Fight it with every thing you have.

In the Kingdom of God, the best way to fight our enemies is by coming against them with an opposite spirit. For example, Jesus taught us to bless those who curse us and to pray for those who despitefully use us. Similarly, the way to destroy fear is through strengthening our faith. As your faith grows stronger your fear will grow weaker. Unfortunately, the reverse also holds true, that as you listen to fear your faith grows weaker so that they counterbalance each other.

So if God is pleased with faith and the devil is pleased with fear the question is how do I strengthen my faith? The apostle Paul said that it comes by hearing the word of God (Romans 10:17). If I want strong faith I must immerse myself in the Word of God—not just read it, but meditate on it. Then when the Word becomes internalized we must stand firmly upon the promises of God, confess His promises, rest upon His promises, and refuse to be moved. Otherwise, fear will come and whisper in your ear, "Maybe God's not going to come through this time." The devil wants us to fear that what God has said in His Word will not come to pass.

Don't be fooled into thinking that all you have to do is to have an anointed Christian lay hands on you to cast out the spirit of fear. Though that may represent a significant part of the solution, if that's all you do the fear will probably leave for only a season. Unless you take the initiative to bathe yourself in the Word, the stronghold of fear will eventually return.

I strongly encourage meditation in the Word. When you read a passage of Scripture stop and pray to God, "Lord please give me this passage. Let these words be engraved in my heart." Open up your heart and allow God's Word to sink into your heart. Another helpful exercise is to visualize Biblical scenes and play them over and over in your mind. Probably the discipline that has been most beneficial in my life is the practice of memorizing Scripture.

I have memorized hundreds of Bible verses and some people ask me if I have a photographic memory. No, it is a matter of focus. I know people who can name the actors in every movie ever filmed while others know all the popular musical performers. I like football but I can't even name the players on my favorite team. Why? Because that's not my passion. Beloved, I urge you to get passionate about the Word of God because there truly is life and freedom in the Word.

Sometimes Scripture passages on the subject of faith don't say what we think they say until we look at them a little more closely. For instance take Mark 11:22. *So Jesus answered and said to them,*

*"Have faith in God."* The preposition "in" is not in the original Greek. The Greek phrase, *exete pistin theou* literally reads "Have faith God." It may be translated "Have the faith **of** God," or "Have God's faith." *Theou*, the word for "God" is in the genitive case in the original language which means that we may add the word "of" or the word "in." If I'm sounding a little technical here hang in there with me because it is of utmost importance that you get this. The genitive case is normally used to describe a noun much like an adjective. The genitive of description lies closest to the root meaning of the genitive case and, thus, a better translation in my opinion would be to use the word "of" rather than "in." "Of" means that it is God's faith and comes from or originates in Him.

Acts 3:16 describes the healing of the lame man at the Beautiful Gate: *And His name, through faith in His name, has made this man strong, whom you see and know. Yes, **the faith which comes through Him** has given him this perfect soundness in the presence of you all* (emphasis added). Peter understood that the faith that he had to heal this man came to him through Jesus and through His Name. Peter received God's faith from Jesus' Name and Jesus' presence as the Holy Spirit came upon him and the lame man.

I like what Mark Virkler says on this subject,

> *Having God's faith means that when I need heart faith which casts mountains into the sea (Mk. 11:22-24), I ask God for this faith since faith is a manifestation of the Holy Spirit (1 Cor. 12:9) Who is in me. I simply say, "God, please release Your faith in my heart." I speak to my heart, "Faith arise, faith arise, faith arise!" And I look and see God expressing Himself and His faith into my heart and out through my being.*
>
> *It becomes God in action out through me, and not me in action. It is not me straining to accomplish believing. It is me asking and receiving, listening to what God is saying – the essence of the faith of Abraham (see Romans 4:16-17 and Genesis 12:1, 4; 22:2-3) – and commanding it forth as Jesus says in Mark*

*11:22-24. These are two completely different postures. I am not striving to believe; I am asking and receiving. These are two completely different pictures in my mind. They bring two completely different results. Striving is religion. Asking and receiving is Christianity. Come, let us ask and receive (Jn. 16:24).* xxx

## Prayer

*Father in heaven, I repent for my lack of diligence in spending time in Your Word. Forgive me for not making it a priority. Bring me to the place where I love Your Word more than anything. Give me the heart of the psalmist who cried out, "I rejoice at Your word, as one who finds great treasure" (Psalm 119:162). Let my spirit be rooted deeply in Your Word. Lord, I recognize that faith is a manifestation of the Holy Spirit Who dwells in me. I ask You to release Your faith in me, in Jesus' name, Amen.*

# 21

---

# Nightmares

*When you lie down, you will not be afraid; yes, you will lie down and your sleep will be sweet.*

(Proverbs 3:24)

Nearly everyone I have ministered to has experienced nightmares, myself included. Where do these dreams come from? When my children were little I learned a valuable lesson in this regard. Simply stated it is this: Certain objects brought into the home can cause bad dreams.

One night my son Jeremy woke us up with a blood-curdling scream. Ruthie and I ran to his bedroom only to see him shaking in fear. As Christian parents we prayed for him until the peace of God filled his room. We thought we took care of the problem but the nightmares persisted. Finally one night after calming him down, I asked God about the cause. The Lord pointed me to an object in his room and led me to remove it. Once I did the nightmares ceased.

There were no more bad dreams, that is, for a season. After several months my daughter, Heather, woke up crying out in fear. Again we did the same thing. We prayed until God's presence filled her room and she was able to sleep peacefully. But the next night the nightmare came back. This time we were a little wiser. I haven't always been the sharpest knife in the drawer when it comes to spiritual matters but I was catching on. We cried out, "God, is there a reason for Heather's bad dreams?" And immediately the Lord brought to mind some Smurf paraphernalia in her room.

Grandmother, with good intentions, had given Heather Smurf sheets for Christmas. With curiosity we viewed this seemingly innocent Saturday morning cartoon. To our horror we witnessed the animated characters lie in a circle on the floor with a pentagram in the middle. Then they proceeded to cast spells. Even with our limited knowledge of the dark side this act was so blatantly occultic in nature we couldn't miss it. Without hesitation we removed all the Smurf toys and effects from our home. Once we did, the nightmares immediately ceased.

Beloved, God does not wish for us to live with nightmares. He wants our sleep to be sweet. If nightmares come we should ask God, "Lord, what are you trying to say to me?" He may direct you to rid your home of an object or artifact that attracts demonic spirits. Please don't go to seed on this teaching and think everything is evil. But when you bring objects into your home that are specifically used by the occult or for worship by a non-Christian religion you give demons permission to come into your home.

Another factor to keep in mind is that your home or land may be defiled due to the actions of people who lived there before you. A murder, suicide, or satanic rituals performed on your property will spiritually pollute the land. Take the initiative to cleanse your home and land by praying around the perimeter of your property.
xxxi

Along this line, when I sleep in a motel or hotel I always bless the room and do some spiritual housecleaning. The reason I do this is because when wicked immoral acts were committed in a hotel room evil spirits gain access and these spirits may affect one's sleep.

I pray a prayer like this: "In the name of Jesus I command every evil spirit that may be in this room to leave now. I have authority over you because I am under Jesus' authority and because I have legal rights to this room. I command you not to return until I have checked out, in Jesus name." This prayer only takes a few seconds and keeps me from restless nights as my human spirit is able to focus on the Lord in peace.

Nightmares may also find their roots in the viewing of horror movies. People who get a thrill out of being scared thrive on these kinds of films. It's a favorite form of entertainment. What is the goal of horror films? Obviously they seek to produce fear. Ask yourself again, "Where does fear come from?" The devil will do anything to plant fearful thoughts in your mind. Satan haunts children with nightmares over something they watched or heard on a TV program, movie, or video game. When mental images of horror get imprinted in our minds Satan has an opening to put fear in us. That's why David said, *I will set nothing wicked before my eyes (Psalm 101:3).* Notice how Isaiah describes those who are right with God: *He who walks righteously and speaks uprightly, he who despises the gain of oppressions, who gestures with his hands, refusing bribes, **who stops his ears from hearing of bloodshed, and shuts his eyes from seeing evil*** (Isaiah 33:15, emphasis mine).

Owning books based on witchcraft or magic also opens the door to the demonic. God gave strict orders not to have anything to do with the dark side: *"There shall not be found among you anyone who makes his son or his daughter to pass through the fire, or one who practices witchcraft, or a soothsayer, or one who interprets omens, or a sorcerer, or one who conjures spells. Or a medium, or a spiritist, or one who calls up the dead"* (Deut. 18:10-11).

If you or your children experience recurring nightmares ask the Lord to reveal the cause. Nightmares may be the result of inner pain and God is speaking about the need of healing in your heart and/or deliverance. Recurring nightmares often completely disappear when a demon of fear is cast out and traumatic memories are healed.

Often nightmares stem from generational curses and have nothing to do with personal trauma or direct involvement with the occult. Scripture admonishes that the sins of the fathers affect their children to the fourth generation. I recommend you seek ministry from a trained deliverance minister to break the evil ties through your bloodline. (Vision Life Ministries offers Biblically sound seminars and one-on-one sessions to break generational curses.)

God wills for you and your family to sleep in peace, so don't settle for anything less. Seek after God's wisdom related to the situation. In fact, the context of the key verse for this chapter has to do with wisdom. James said it this way, *If any of you lacks wisdom, let him ask of God* (James 1:5a).

## Prayer

*Father, show me if I have given the enemy access to my heart or home. Are there any wounds of my heart that need healing? Help me to find the right person to break generational curses at work in my life. I ask You for Your wisdom that I might walk in Your ways because I want Your sweet sleep. I pray in Jesus' name, Amen.*

# 22

# Perfectionism

*To the praise of the glory of his grace, by which He made us accepted in the Beloved.*

(Ephesians 1:6)

Allen prided himself in his ability to get things done right. He felt that he needed to give more than 100% to every project his boss assigned and he usually took it hard when flaws were pointed out in his work. He perceived that his co-workers were able to achieve success with a minimum amount of effort while making fewer mistakes–so he determined that he just needed to try harder to make up the difference. Allen learned early in life that other people valued him when he accomplished something or achieved success so he made up his mind that he would be the best in everything he did.

Allen is a classic perfectionist. To perfectionists their unhealthy striving is rarely perceived as a fault. Instead, they get the idea that the reason they are so successful is because they *are* perfectionists. The truth is, however, that this behavior does not lead to success. If they become successful it is in spite of, not because of, the unrealistic pressure they place on themselves. Another misconception is that they are the "go to person" if you want something done right. In reality, perfectionists commonly procrastinate and miss deadlines because they are striving to make their projects flawless. Still another myth is that they have a desire to please others. To the contrary, they display perfectionist tendencies in order to win love, acceptance and approval.

At this point you might be wondering why a chapter on perfectionism is included in a book on fear. That is because, although it is based on a low sense of self esteem, perfectionism can also be seen as another form of fear. Some of the main causes include fear of failure, fear of making mistakes, fear of inadequacy and fear of disapproval.

Perfectionists tend to set unreachable goals. They inevitably fail to meet their goals because the goals were unrealistic to begin with. They feel like what they accomplish is never quite good enough. They strive to give more than 100% on everything they do but, consequently, they become self-critical and self-blaming, which leads to anxiety and depression. They become overly sensitive when criticized.

What can be done about this malady? First, recognize it for what it is. Perfectionism is not your friend—it will take you down the road to frustration and alienation. Second, confront the fears behind the perfectionism. Ask yourself, "What am I really afraid of? What is the worst thing that can happen?" Then, set realistic reasonable goals and try giving a little less than 100%. Relax, give yourself a break. You may be trying to be perfect rather than working toward success. Next, learn to see your mistakes as springboards to growth and learning. With this mindset you can actually celebrate your failures and thereby feel good about yourself.

And lastly, meditate on the truth that your self-worth is not determined by your performance. God loves you and he has accepted you just the way you are as long as you are "in the beloved," as our key verse states. If you are in Christ and He is in you then God loves you the same way He loves His Son. Get your self-esteem from what God says about you, not from how well you perform. Perfectionism is based on the lie that says you will be accepted, approved and appreciated if you excel in every task you undertake.

## Prayer

*Father in heaven, I recognize that perfectionism is wicked, ungodly and against You. Please forgive me. I renounce perfectionism. I repent of it and break any agreement I ever made with it. In Jesus' name I command all perfectionism to leave me now and go to dry places. I bring all my thoughts into captivity to the obedience of Christ, in the name of Jesus, Amen.*

# 23

---

# Phobias

*The wicked flee when no man pursues, but the righteous are bold as a lion.*

(Proverbs 28:1)

P hobias are irrational fears about people, places, and things.[xxxii] They are extremely common and often debilitating. For years my friend, Roni, suffered from the fear of heights. Phobias often start in childhood, however, Roni's acrophobia may have come into being sometime during adulthood but I'm not sure exactly when. Here is her testimony:

*"All my life, I always had a fear of heights—not to the point of being completely debilitating, but to the degree that if I had to climb a ladder or get on the roof my legs were spaghetti and my stomach was in knots. I would force myself to do what needed to be done, but it was a very uncomfortable experience. Driving on an overpass was terrible. I would fix my eyes on the road ahead and dare not look to either side. By the time*

*I reached the other side I was shaking inside. More than once, I had to go up on a tower or tall building (usually at the prodding of others, just to prove I could). But I stayed with my back to the wall, shaking in fear. I didn't dare go near the rail or enjoy the view.*

*"A few years ago I went through a rather dramatic inner healing and deliverance. Of course immediately I noticed the obvious sense of peace and wholeness that follows deliverance. However, I didn't realize until some weeks later that I no longer had a fear of heights. I was driving somewhere and I drove over a huge overpass. It wasn't until I was on the other side that I realized, 'Hey, that didn't bother me at all.' The thought occurred to me that I had been delivered from a spirit of fear. In order to test the theory, I took my daughter the next day to Six Flags. We went to the top of their lookout tower. I was walking all around, looking over the edge and praising God for my deliverance."*

What a blessing it is to Roni to be free!

What seems funny to some can be an absolute terror to the one plagued with a phobia. I'll never forget the time when I was a child of 8 or 9 years of age. I went to Indiana to visit my father and his wife. My stepbrother, Larry asked me to go out in the back yard with his friend. They had trapped some mice in a mason jar and told me to take them inside to show Ma. Innocently, I took the rodents in the kitchen where she was working, hoping she would be pleased with my treasure. To my astonishment, she jumped up on top of the kitchen table and commenced to scream at the top of her lungs. Dumbfounded, I didn't know what to do except stand there holding the jar of mice while she danced on the table, red-faced and frantic. Finally, she composed herself enough to shout, "Get them out of here!!" I'm sure Larry didn't think it was funny once Ma got a hold of him.

Some of the most common phobias include the fear of spiders

(arachnophobia) fear of snakes (ophidiophobia), fear of dogs (cynophobia), fear of open, public places (agoraphobia), fear of heights (acrophobia), fear of closed in spaces (claustrophobia), fear of water (aquaphobia), fear of the dark (achluophobia), fear of lightning (astrapophobia), fear of flying (aviatophobia), fear of dentists (dentophobia), fear of microbes (microphobia), fear of choking or smothering (pnigerophobia), fear of germs (spermatophobia), and fear of your mother-in-law. I'm just joking about the last one but there really is a classified fear known as (novercaphobia) or literally, fear of your mother-in-law.

There are at least two factors involved in treating a phobia effectively: first, confronting the fear, and second, dealing with any associated frightening thoughts. It is important to stop avoiding the fear. I used to have acrophobia but when I ran away from being in high places it only made the phobia intensify. When I cut class in high school rather than give a required speech it caused the fear of public speaking to become paralyzing.

Learn to face your fears. However, it helps to do so whilst managing the level of anxiety because it can be overwhelming to start in the midst of the feared situation. Modern psychology suggests the approach of a graded exposure. Start with an aspect of the fear that is the least threatening and work your way up. For example, somebody with a phobia of mice might use the following progression:

1. Reading about mice,
2. Looking at and then touching a photograph of a mouse,
3. Looking at/touching a toy mouse,
4. Looking at/touching a jar with a live small mouse in it,
5. Picking the mouse out of the jar,
6. Picking up a large mouse.

I recommend that you get in a relaxed position listening to soft worship music and breathe deeply. One exercise that helps me relax is to imagine that there are nostrils just below my belly button and then I breathe in from my diaphragm. After becoming relaxed, focus on one stage at a time and stay in each stage until the anxiety is gone. Don't escape when the anxiety is high because this only reinforces the fear. Allow up to 20-30 minutes for each stage because the anxiety will diminish and eventually disappear if you stay in the situation. You will begin to learn that you can survive, and even remain calm, in the situation that used to cause fear.[xxxiii] I recommend a good licensed, Biblically based, Christian counselor to help walk you through the process.

I used to be terrified of public speaking (problematic for one who is called to be a pastor). The way I overcame it was to just do it. I began by speaking in front of small audiences at an outreach center for alcoholics and drug addicts. In their broken condition I knew they would not be critiquing my sermons and this realization took away the intimidation. Gradually I grew in confidence and reliance on the Spirit of the Lord to anoint my preaching so that speaking in churches did not fill me with overwhelming fear.

Remember that fear is **F**alse **E**vidence **A**ppearing **R**eal, that is to say, a phobia is based on a lie. That's what strongholds are made of–lies. With this in mind, the next thing you can do is identify the threatening thoughts associated with your phobia. Then try to write them down and challenge them with the truth. Ask the Holy Spirit to speak truth to you regarding the lie. For example, if you have the fear of flying, ask the Lord to help you identify the lie. The lie might be, "The plane is going to crash." Then ask Him to reveal His truth about the situation. He may remind you that flying is statistically the safest way to travel. He may say, "Even if the plane crashes I promised never to leave you or forsake you. You will always be in My presence."

Anxiety is a common human phenomenon and it won't harm you—the worst it can do is make you feel very unpleasant. Each time you confront your fear, face it in praise and thanksgiving, thanking God for another opportunity to learn how to overcome your phobia, rather than something to dread. When the fear is gone make sure to praise and thank the Lord some more for the victory.

## Prayer

*Father in heaven, I repent for having come into agreement with the fear of _____(name the fear). I receive Your forgiveness and the blood of Jesus cleanses me now. And now fear of _____(name the fear) I renounce you, I reject you, and I break any agreement I ever made with you. In the name of Jesus, I command you to leave me now and go to dry places. Father, help me to face my fears and rely on Your power to enable me to overcome. Thank You Jesus, that You defeated fear when You died on the cross and rose again. Thank You for the abiding presence of the Holy Spirit to help me do what I cannot do in my own strength. I pray in Jesus' name, Amen.*

# 24

## The Fear of the Retaliation of the Enemy

*Then the seventy returned with joy, saying, "Lord, even
the demons are subject to us in Your name." And He said
to them, "I saw Satan fall like lightning from heaven.
Behold, I give you the authority to trample on serpents
and scorpions, and over all the power of the enemy, and
nothing shall by any means hurt you."
(Luke 10: 17-19)*

There have been many times that I have experienced the
enemy's attempt to sidetrack me as I was preparing to teach
and minister deliverance. One time, just before I was scheduled
to teach a seminar, two air conditioners went out on the same day–
one in my home and one in my truck. When the air conditioner
in my truck went out I realized that this inconvenience was no
coincidence and that this distraction was the work of the enemy. To
my delight the problem was quickly solved when I took authority
over any spirits hindering my vehicle and commanded them to
get their hands off my air conditioner. When I did, immediately
the air conditioner began to work and we had no problems with it

for years. In retrospect I wish I had done the same thing with my home air conditioner system.

I can think of another time when a young man was on his way to meet me for a ministry session. A few minutes before our scheduled appointment he called me on the phone. With stress in his voice he revealed that the engine in his car mysteriously died while he was driving down the street and that he had tried and tried to start it again with no success. He was about 20 minutes away and had decided that the reasonable thing to do was to cancel our meeting so he could tend to his car. I said, "Before we do that let's do something." I took authority over any evil spirits responsible and bound and broke their power over his engine. Then I said, "Try to start it again." This time, to his amazement, the car started right away and he made it to the church and was only a few minutes late for our appointment.

Richard says he wishes he knew as a young pastor what he knows now. Here is his story:

*"One of the greatest lessons I have learned in the area of the enemy's retaliation is when I was the senior pastor of a church in northern California. After attending a three-day prayer conference in the San Francisco area, I went back to my church with an excitement and zeal for a prayer ministry to be established with the men in our congregation.*

*Most of our men had to be at work early and were tied up in the evening so we planned a daily prayer meeting, Monday through Friday, at 5:30 AM. I enlisted a good size group of men and in our first prayer session we experienced the power of God. It proved to be a glorious time in the Lord! We looked ahead with great expectations as to how God would use us as we met together in powerful believing prayer.*

*The only problem was that the night before I could not get to sleep. So all of that day I was dragging. My repeated thoughts were, "I'm so tired. I'm going to hit the sack early and sleep like a baby tonight." But try to imagine my frustration when I went to bed that evening and as soon as my head hit the pillow my eyes went open and I was wide awake. So I went another night without sleep but I was determined to be faithful to our prayer meeting. Consequently that day my energy level was even lower. I kept thinking, 'I am so exhausted there is no way I will stay awake tonight.' All day I was looking forward to a good night's rest. I was so very tired, but strangely, as soon as my head hit the pillow, I was awake and alert.*

*After about a week of this pattern and feeling completely drained, I began to make excuses for not showing up to prayer. Before long the men's prayer meeting ceased to exist. What I didn't know then but know now was that all believing prayer is warfare and the enemy hates it when God's people pray. He will do all that he can to discourage us from coming together to pray. In our case he used sleeplessness to put an end to that which was disrupting his kingdom. At that time in my life I didn't possess the knowledge to know how to handle that frustrating situation but it did show me that there are often repercussions brought on by the enemy when we step out in obedience to God."*

Oh, yes, my friend, the devil will fight to put an end to all that weakens his kingdom. But we need not fear his attacks for, *Greater is he that is in you that he that is in the world* (1 John 4:4). When Jesus came to earth He destroyed the power of the enemy. See what the Word of God says in 1 John 3:8 out of the Amplified Version: *The reason the Son of God was made manifest (visible) was to undo (destroy, loosen, and dissolve) the works the devil [has done].*

Many people refuse to use their rightful authority to bring deliverance in the lives of hurting friends and family for fear that the kingdom of darkness will retaliate. As one pastor foolishly said, "I have made a pact with the devil–I will leave him alone if he will leave me alone." Although it is true that Satan will do his best to silence those who speak out against him, this pastor's approach to spiritual warfare does not line up with the example of Christ.

One time Jesus sent out seventy of his disciples two-by-two into the city and place where He Himself was about to go. He instructed them to heal the sick and to proclaim the gospel of the Kingdom of God.

At the conclusion of these mission trips the Bible says, *Then the seventy returned with joy, saying, "Lord, even the demons are subject to us in Your name."* It thrilled the disciples to witness demons departing from poor hurting people, that they had the authority to expel darkness in Jesus' name. But keep in mind, the devil hates it when his dark kingdom is disturbed.

So Jesus responded by saying, *"I saw Satan fall like lightning from heaven,"* signifying that the devil was defeated. Jesus goes on to say, *"Behold, I give you the authority to trample on serpents and scorpions, and over all the power of the enemy, and nothing shall by any means hurt you"* (Luke 10:19). So our Lord was teaching that the enemy cannot hurt us through retaliation after we have performed the works of God. Satan is a defeated foe.

The enemy targeted the disciples out of retaliation in order to put an end to their deliverance ministry. But Jesus encourages them by saying, *". . . and nothing shall by any means hurt you."*

You may be thinking, "How can this be true? You just gave several examples of Satan's power to hinder the ministry of the servant of God." Though it seems to contradict, we need to take a closer look at the word *hurt* in verse 19. This doesn't mean that Satan has no power to cause us harm, to distract us, or to damper the fire of our ministry. You see, the only real hurt is that which hurts our heart. Satan may afflict us but he cannot hurt our human spirit unless we give him permission. In fact, when Satan attacks, if we respond the right way, it only serves to strengthen us and develop our character. The godly response is that we rely on the grace of God to see us through.

This is why Jesus goes on to say, *"Nevertheless do not rejoice in this, that the spirits are subject to you, but rather rejoice because your names are written in heaven"* (Luke 10:20). This is to say that no real harm can come to you if you are a true believer because your name is written in heaven. Try as he may, the devil cannot pry you out of the Father's hand.

Keep in mind that, though we have authority over the enemy, he still can afflict and harass us. But the good news is, he cannot *hurt* us or destroy us. The apostle Paul prayed three times that the "thorn in his flesh," a messenger of Satan, would be removed from his life. But God didn't remove that thorn. Instead, He used it to develop Paul's character and to teach him that God's grace is sufficient.

So what if my air conditioner was not miraculously fixed? What if the young man's engine had not been instantaneously repaired? Then God's grace would have been sufficient if I would only believe it and rest in the Lord. Yes, there are plenty of times that Satan will leave our circumstances when we take our authority over him and in this we rejoice. Realistically, however, sometimes those thorns are allowed to remain to be used of God to develop our character. In this we should also rejoice because our names are written in heaven.

# Prayer

*Father in heaven, I agree with You that fear is sin. Please forgive me for fearing what the enemy might do to me for serving You. I thank You Lord that Jesus has already defeated the devil. I will walk in Your victory knowing that You will protect me, in Jesus' name, Amen.*

# 25

---

# Fear⊁Faith

*For whatever is not from faith is sin.*

(Romans 14:23b)

When my son Jeremy was five years old we went to visit Ruthie's mother in Southern California. After a full day at Disneyland we returned to grandma's house to get some much-needed sleep. A little after midnight we woke up to a blood-curdling scream. We rushed to the room where the kids had bedded down and, to our horror, we saw that my son had fallen out of the top bunk and hit his arm on the dresser. The shattered bone of his upper left arm protruded through the muscle and skin and he lay in a pool of blood.

Someone quickly called 911 and I knelt down on the floor with Jeremy to keep him calm and to pray for him. Miraculously the bleeding stopped by the time the paramedics arrived.

After we got to the nearest hospital a bone specialist was called to perform emergency surgery. When the orthopedic surgeon arrived and examined our son he came into the waiting room to talk to us. He said, "Mr. and Mrs. Frye, this is the worst break of this kind that I have ever seen in all my years of being a surgeon. I don't know if we will be able to save his arm. And even if we can, he may never be able to use his arm because it looks like the nerve damage is severe."

Ruthie, her mom, and I anxiously sat in the waiting room where we prayed for healing and a successful surgery. After a season of prayer the two ladies started to chitchat and enter into light-hearted conversation. Nervously, I scolded them saying, "Why are you just talking when you should be praying?" Now, that statement may sound admirable and noble, but the truth is, I was more motivated by fear than I was by faith in the power of God. This exemplifies what is known as fear-faith.

Fear-faith looks very godly. Fear-faith motivates us to do religious activities that give the impression that we are committed and consecrated to God. Actually, when we let fear motivate us we enter into sin because the Bible says, *For whatsoever is without faith is sin* (Romans 14:23b).

By the grace of God and in spite of my unbelief all went well with Jeremy's surgery and eventually he regained full use of his arm. He went on to play the piano and compete in football for which we gave God the praise. But when he played football I always prayed a lot before each of his games that he would be safe. Again, fear-faith set in. Fear motivated me to pray earnestly and long, but on the outside it looked like faith.

When we pray in faith it pleases God because without faith it is impossible to please Him. Jesus said, "When the Son of God returns will He find faith on the earth?" Jesus didn't say He'd be looking for much prayer. What impresses Him is faith.

Instead of continuing to beg and plead with God to heal and protect Jeremy when he had his surgery, it would have been better to express thanksgiving and praise. When we praise God it releases faith. A more powerful prayer would be, "Father I thank You for Your power that is being released right now to protect and heal his arm. Thank You for healing him now. Praise You Lord that You are the great physician."

Remember to stand on the promises of God. We need to remind God and ourselves of His promises by speaking them out loud. This is a powerful form of prayer that releases faith. Without remembering God's promises it is easy to let fear in our hearts, even while we're praying.

## Prayer

*Forgive me, Father, for praying or doing other religious things out of fear. I agree with You that fear is sin no matter what it looks like on the outside. I reject and renounce fear-faith and command it to leave me now, in Jesus' name, Amen.*

# 26

---

# Fear of Wasted Years

*Brethren, I do not count myself to have apprehended; but one thing I do, forgetting those things which are behind and reaching forward to those things which are ahead, I press toward the goal for the prize of the upward call of God in Christ Jesus.*

(Philippians 3:13-14)

People often come to me who are plagued with the fear that they have wasted their years so far and that they will never fulfill what God called them to do. I like to remind them that Moses didn't even start his ministry until he was eighty years old. God used Smith Wigglesworth in a mighty way to heal and bring untold numbers into the Kingdom. Yet this spiritual giant didn't begin his ministry until he was in his 50's!

I had a friend, Paul Priddy, who is now gone to be with the Lord who was the greatest personal soul winner I've ever known. One year he led over a thousand people to accept Jesus as Lord and Savior on a one-on-one basis. Wherever he went he talked to people about Jesus and had a unique way of communicating the gospel. He was also a mighty prayer warrior and God performed signs and wonders through him. Yet he did not begin his ministry until he was in his 60's!

Not everyone is called to be a Smith Wigglesworth or a Paul Priddy but all of us have a personal destiny. It's not too late to fulfill your purpose in life and join God in His plan for you. Don't believe the lie that you've missed your opportunity to get on track with God's design for you.

Forget about the past and start anew in pressing in to follow hard after God. Focus on your relationship with Him. Out of that intimacy will flow everything you need to do. Remember, God has created us to be human beings, not human doings. The main reason God created us is that we might have fellowship with Him.

## Prayer

*Father in heaven, please forgive me for bowing down to the kingdom of darkness by listening to the fear of wasted years. Today is the beginning of the rest of my life so I reject and renounce this fear. I command it to leave me now and go to dry places, in Jesus' name, Amen.*

# 27

---

# Fear and Envy/Jealousy

*Let your conduct be without covetousness, and be content with such things as you have. For He Himself has said, "I will never leave you nor forsake you." So we may boldly say: "The LORD is my helper; I will not fear. What can man do to me?"*

(Hebrews 13:5-6)

E nvy and jealousy open a person up to a host of tormenting problems. First, envy/jealousy leads to strife. Scripture repeatedly ties envy and strife together: *Let us walk properly as in the day, not in revelry and drunkenness, not in licentiousness and lewdness, not in **strife** and **envy*** (Romans 13:13, emphases mine). *For you are still **carnal**. For where there are **envy, strife**, and divisions among you, are you not carnal and behaving like mere men?* (1 Corinthians 3:3). *He is proud, knowing nothing, but is obsessed with disputes and arguments over words, from which come **envy, strife**, reviling, evil suspicions* (1 Timothy 6:4, emphases mine). Envy and strife go together. Therefore, if there is strife in your life, look for envy.

Second, some health problems can be traced to the spiritual root of envy/jealousy: *A sound heart is life to the body, but envy is rottenness to the bones* (Proverbs 14:30). The immune system has its origin in the bone marrow and envy/jealousy will weaken your body's ability to fight off disease. Scripture teaches that you will live longer if you avoid covetousness (a form of envy/ jealousy). *But he who hates covetousness will prolong his days* (Proverbs 28:16b).

Covetousness is actually a form of envy/jealousy and covetousness will cause you to miss out on your spiritual inheritance: *For this you know, that no fornicator, unclean person, nor covetous man, who is an idolater, has any inheritance in the kingdom of Christ and God* (Ephesians 5:5). God has great blessings in store for His children but envy/jealousy will keep us from receiving.

In addition, envy may bring confusion. *But if you have bitter envy and self-seeking in your hearts, do not boast and lie against the truth. This wisdom does not descend from above, but is earthly, sensual, demonic. For where envy and self-seeking exist, confusion and every evil thing will be there* (James 3:14-16). Do you have confusion in your life? Look for envy.

Another problem with envy/jealousy is that it produces bitterness. When Joseph's brothers experienced the preferential treatment meted out by their father, their hearts brimmed with envy: *And his brothers envied him* (Genesis 37:11a). Sadly, their envy turned to bitterness and they conspired to kill Joseph. Later the oldest brother convinced them not to commit murder so instead they ended up selling him into slavery. Then they lied to their father implying that a wild animal killed Joseph. The writer of Hebrews warns us of the consequences of bitterness: *Looking diligently lest anyone fall short of the grace of God; lest any root of bitterness springing up cause trouble, and by this many become defiled* (Hebrews 12:15).

Even though it wreaks so much havoc in our lives, the tragic truth is that few people recognize when they walk in the spirit of envy/ jealousy. In over 30 years of ministry I finally had one person come to me for pastoral counseling asking for help with envy/ jealousy. I congratulated her that she was the first to seek my help in overcoming this stronghold. I suppose it is rare for us to acknowledge this sin, in part, due to the fact that we are ashamed to admit when it's operating in us. This sin seems so petty and childish when brought out into the open so we tend to play it down or try to ignore it. But God thinks it is so important to deal with that He made one of His Ten Commandments address the subject: *"Thou shalt not covet,"* and remember that covetousness is a form of envy/jealousy.

Since so much is at stake it behooves us to investigate the dynamics of this sin. Envy and jealousy come in through the fear of loss. In Hebrews 13:5-6 we read, *Let your conduct be without covetousness; be content with such things as you have. For He Himself has said, "I will never leave you nor forsake you." So we may boldly say: "The LORD is my helper; I will not fear. What can man do to me?"* Do you see the connection God places between envy/jealousy and fear?

When Saul heard the women singing, *"Saul has slain his thousands and David his ten thousand,"* Saul was obviously envious and jealous. But the scripture says in that context that he was afraid of David. Interestingly, the Lord refers to fear in that context at least four different times. Why? Because envy/jealousy often originates with fear or fear of loss, to be more accurate.

The religious leaders delivered Jesus to Pontius Pilate out of envy (Matthew 27:18). They feared that His growing popularity would cause them to lose their influence over the masses. Again we see an example that the fear of loss leads to envy.

Because of our society's twisted values, women often struggle with envy/jealousy when they see another woman whom they perceive to be prettier, better dressed, and shapelier. The emotion behind the envy/jealousy is fear—fear that they will go unnoticed—fear that they will not be appreciated or recognized—fear that they will lose their value. This fear then leads to self-bitterness.

How do you know if envy/jealousy is operating in your life? Sharon, a struggling single mom, belonged to a cell group sponsored by her church that met weekly in homes. At each meeting they shared a meal, sang Christian songs, studied the Bible, and prayed for each other's needs. The custom involved a rotation whereby they took turns holding the gatherings in a different member's home every week. Sharon loved the support and fellowship her small group provided but she also enjoyed the aspect of seeing the inside of the beautiful homes in the upscale community where the church was located.

Sharon was always the first one to compliment the host on her lovely home. "Oh, you have a beautiful home," she often remarked enthusiastically. "God has really blessed you!" But inwardly, Sharon was thinking, "This is very nice, but what about me?" What was Sharon wrestling with? A spirit of envy/ jealousy. And what was this demon doing? It was robbing her of her joy. Rather than being content and grateful for what she had, fear began to get ahold in her heart that God was withholding something good—fear that she had lost God's favor.

Ivor was a decent musician. Although his skills were limited he played the piano well enough and possessed an above average voice. The mission church he attended quickly enlisted him to lead the worship team on Sunday mornings. The music program went well during the fledgling first couple of years as the church became established. As the church grew, gradually other more capable musicians volunteered their services.

One day a new recruit was asked to play the keyboard and sing a solo during Sunday morning worship. It was immediately obvious to all that he was a highly gifted musician with a special anointing for bringing the congregation into an awesome awareness of the presence of God. Before the pastor started his sermon that morning he heaped lavish praise upon the special music. Then after the service while people fellowshipped in the foyer, one by one members approached Ivor mentioning how much they enjoyed the special music and wished the individual would perform again soon.

Ivor smiled, agreeing with their assessment, but inwardly discomfort gnawed at his insides. Thoughts raced through his mind such as, "I work hard volunteering my services week after week and where is the thanks I get?" Ivor was battling envy, a common phenomenon amongst musicians. If it bothers you when other people receive the praise for doing the same things you do, then you are struggling with a spirit of envy/jealousy. If you feel threatened when someone comes along who is more highly gifted than you in the area of your expertise, than envy/jealousy more than likely presents a problem for you.

Another way to discern envy is to ask yourself if you often make comparisons. Do you tend to compare your income, talents, education, or accomplishments with that of others?

The apostle Paul had this to say about comparisons: *For we dare not class ourselves or compare ourselves with those who commend themselves. But they, measuring themselves by themselves, and comparing themselves among themselves, are not wise* (2 Corinthians 10:12). It is foolish to seek self-worth by making comparisons because there will always be people better looking, more intelligent, wealthier, more talented, and more successful. Our self-worth comes from God's estimation. He promised to never leave us nor forsake us. Therefore, we must have great value to Him just the way we are.

I encourage you to take a spiritual inventory. If you often experience confusion and strife in your life the root cause may be envy/jealousy. If there is a problem with your immune system the spiritual basis may be envy/jealousy. If you struggle with lack of contentment and joy or unresolved anger, the root may be traced back to envy/jealousy. If you tend to compare yourself to others, look for envy/jealousy. It would be wise for you to ask God to reveal any envy/jealousy that might be lurking in the recesses of your heart. Recognition is 90% of the victory when dealing with any stronghold. But envy is so subtle it takes the illuminating power of the Holy Spirit to enable us to see it.

Don't go into morbid introspection or conjure up something that is not really there. But if God reveals that you are disposed to harbor envy/jealousy in your life, I encourage you to pray the following prayer.

## Prayer

*Heavenly Father, I agree with You that envy/jealousy/ covetousness is sin and I repent. This sin is wicked, ungodly, and against You. Because of this sin I rightfully deserve death on a cross. But I thank You Lord Jesus that You died in my place. I receive Your forgiveness. The blood of Jesus cleanses me now and I am free, I am forgiven. Please bring this fleshly tendency to death at the cross of Christ. And now envy/jealousy/covetousness, I reject you, I renounce you, and I break any agreement I ever made with you. I command you to leave me now and go to dry places, in the name of Jesus Christ, Amen.*

# 28

# Fear and Divination

*Now it happened, as we went to prayer, that a certain slave girl possessed with a spirit of divination met us, who brought her masters much profit by fortune-telling. This girl followed Paul and us, and cried out, saying, "These men are the servants of the Most High God, who proclaim to us the way of salvation." And this she did for many days. But Paul, greatly annoyed, turned and said to the spirit, "I command you in the name of Jesus Christ to come out of her." And he came out that very hour.*

(Acts 16:16-18)

*Also, many of those who had practiced magic brought their books together and burned them in the sight of all.*

(Acts 19:19a)

It is impossible to rid your life of fear if you have not dealt with the spirit of divination. Fear and the spirit of divination weave themselves together to hold each other in place. Divination fuels fear and fear fuels divination. Fear pushes a person into divination and fear is also a byproduct of divination.

Jeanie's husband, Ron, was diagnosed with an aggressive inoperable brain tumor and was given a maximum of two months to live. She asked her church to put Ron's name on the prayer chain. After word got out about their crisis, an acquaintance told Jeanie about a psychic healer in Mexico who was famous for miraculous cures. The healer often used an unsterilized knife and performed operations while in a trance-like state. The incisions she made healed almost immediately and she had a high success rate with terminal cases. Jeanie's heart told her something was wrong but out of desperation and fear she packed the car and drove her husband to the little town just across the boarder. "After all," she reasoned, "The prayer chain hasn't worked so far and God must somehow be involved in guiding the psychic healer because only God can heal." Fear drove her to do something her heart said was wrong.

Unfortunately, the church in America, by-and-large, is devoid of supernatural power. Consequently, people are drawn to the occult because there they find the supernatural manifestations to help them cope with life. Psychic healing, even though it may produce results, stands in contradiction to the Word of God. Should Christians involve themselves in various forms of divination simply because they work? Occult practices may work but they bring with them new fears that the practitioner never bargained for.

The Bible strictly forbids all practices that relate to divination. When the children of Israel prepared to take possession of the Promised Land God gave this warning: *"When you come into the land which the LORD your God is giving you, you shall not learn to follow the abominations of those nations. There shall not be found among you anyone who makes his son or his daughter pass through the fire, or one who practices witchcraft, or a soothsayer, or one who interprets omens, or a sorcerer, or one who conjures spell, or a medium, or a spiritist, or one who calls up the dead. For all who do these things are an abomination to the LORD, and because of these abominations the LORD your God drives them out from before you. You shall be blameless before the LORD your God. For these nations which you will dispossess listened to soothsayers and diviners; but as for you, the LORD your God has not appointed such for you"* (Deuteronomy 18:9-14).

Unfortunately many Christians open the door to evil influences unintentionally because of lack of knowledge in this area. Satan doesn't care if you innocently play with something related to divination. But when you do you give him permission to gain a certain amount of leverage in your life. For example, many children play with the magic eight ball not realizing that this is a form of divination. Others, out of curiosity, read their horoscope without taking it seriously. It doesn't matter whether or not you believe in astrology. What counts is that you gave the devil legal ground and you need to remove it through repentance and renunciation.

Here is a list of evidences that point to divination at work in your life. Sometimes people inherit a propensity toward divination through the sins of their ancestors. Circle any that you have done at any time in your life whether you did them as an adult or a child. Also circle any you know of that your parents, grandparents, or great grandparents were involved in because the effects of these things get passed on for at least four generations.

| | |
|---|---|
| independence | drugs |
| palm readers | séances |
| games (Masters of the | Freemasonry or secret |
| Universe, Dungeons & | organizations |
| Dragons, Magic Eight Ball, | channeling |
| Pokemon, etc.) | rebellion |
| stubbornness | mediums |
| Ouija boards | crystal balls |
| mutterer (one who talks with a | horoscopes |
| spirit as if talking to himself) | mysticism |

| | |
|---|---|
| unscriptural attempts at | diviners (witches) |
| deliverance (Those that do not | astrology |
| line up with the Word) | fortune-tellers |
| Eastern religions | white witchcraft |
| Satanism (worship of Satan) | tarot cards[xxxiv] |
| TM | |

To this list I would like to add yoga because I am disturbed to see so many Christians involved in this counterfeit attempt to gain peace. Those who promote yoga say that it facilitates peace and inner tranquility. I believe that it does just the opposite. Several knowledgeable people have told me that their experience is that those who continue to practice this ancient form of Hinduism actually find it increasingly more difficult to resist stress. This is because any unscriptural attempt to achieve peace gives the enemy an inroad.

Read carefully the following quotations to help you understand the heart of the problem. Yoga is clearly a form or an expression of religion.

> *"As we have said, many who recommend yoga claim it is an excellent way in which to loosen one's muscles, keep fit, and maintain health. For these people, yoga is simply physical exercise and nothing more; the practice has little to do with religion. Such persons, however, do not properly understand the nature and purpose of true yoga practice. Yoga is much more than merely an innocent form of relaxing the mind and body. One reason that yoga clearly belongs in the category of religion is because the classic yoga texts reveal that proper yoga practice incorporates many goals of occultism. Allegedly, it will not only result in a 'sound' mind and a 'healthy' body, but also in spiritual (occult) enlightenment."[xxxv]*

The physical exercises of yoga are believed to prevent diseases and maintain health through the regulation of prana or mystical life energy. David Fetcho, an authority in yoga theory and practice, states:

*"Physical yoga, according to its classical definitions, is inheritably and functionally incapable of being separated from Eastern religious metaphysics. The Western practitioner who attempts to do so is operating in ignorance and danger, from the yogi's viewpoint, as well as from the Christian."* [xxxvi]

The doctrine of kundalini should also raise some concerns.

*"In Hindu mythology, the serpent goddess kundalini 'rests' at the base of the spine. She is aroused by yoga practice, travels up the spine while regulating prana and opening the body's alleged psychic centers (chakras), finally reaching the top (crown) chakra, permitting the merging of Shiva/Shakti and occult enlightenment."* [xxxvii]

I don't know about you but I don't want a serpent goddess traveling up my back!

Activating the Kundalini is not, as commonly thought, restricted to hatha yoga. Yoga authorities themselves have said that all yoga is fundamentally kundalini yoga and that yoga is senseless without it. This is why no less an authority that Hans Reiker concludes, "Kundalini is the mainstay of all yoga practices." [xxxviii]

Yoga is used as a basic means of achieving an altered state of consciousness.

*"Altered states of consciousness (ASCs) in a New Age context comprise unusual conditions of perception achieved by the deliberate cultivation of often abnormal mental states, states not normally experienced apart from specific religious techniques and/or occult programs."* [xxxix]

The amygdala, the part of the brain that places you in space gets shut down during an altered state of consciousness. When this happens you will experience a feeling of being without boundaries.

Most people believe that Yoga is merely a program for teaching proper breathing and stretching techniques. In actuality, it is designed to produce a mystical experience. Earnest L. Rossi of the Department of Psychology at UCLA asserts that yoga is designed to induce altered states of consciousness.

*"If one considers the ancient yoga science of pranayama (controlled breathing) to have relevance, then one must admit that the manual manipulation of the nasal cycle during meditation (dhyana) is the most thoroughly documented of techniques for altering consciousness. For thousands of years these techniques for the subtle alterations of nasal breathing have been gradually codified into classical texts..."* [xl]

The goal of the yogi is the realization that all is one—in other words, no boundaries. This tenet represents a world view, known as monism, is contrary to Scripture and undermines the teaching of the gospel. Jesus came to save us from our sins so that we might be brought into relationship with God. He didn't come to merely enlighten us. The consequences for involvement in yoga are that the door gets opened to evil spirits, one is easily influenced by surroundings, and one takes on the physical symptoms and mind states of other people. *He that has no rule over his own spirit is like a city that is broken down, and without walls* (Proverbs 25:28).

Other divination practices exist that need to be renounced and repented of. They include but are not limited to the use of pendulums in foretelling the future, tea leaves, fetishes, charms, psychic readings, table tipping, levitation, clairvoyance, ESP, "third eye," mental telepathy, mantras, the use of spirit guides, communication with the dead, out of body experiences, astral projection, Druidism, automatic handwriting, metaphysics, mysticism, spiritism, worship of ancestral spirits, belief in reincarnation, idolatry, consulting with witch doctors, shamanism,

Santeria, psychic healers, New Age doctrine, magic, white magic, black magic, voodoo, traiteur, sorcery, water witching, casting spells, incantations, curses, hexes, vexes, ungodly vows and oaths, ungodly covenants, blood sacrifices, animal sacrifices, human sacrifices, control, intimidation, manipulation, and domination.

In addition, one of the most insidious forms of divination is Freemasonry. Those who join its ranks usually do not understand the full extent of the evil revealed in the higher degrees. Once a Freemason reaches the 33rd degree he learns that the "Great Architect of the Universe" is none other than Lucifer himself. People often protest when I teach on this subject. "My grandfather was a Mason and he was a good person." My response to that objection is "He may have been a good person, but he was deceived in this area." I do not deny that Masons do a lot of good.

As a little boy Clyde badly burned his leg. The doctors did their best but after months of treatment they said they would have to amputate. Then someone on his behalf contacted the Shriners, a Masonic organization that does much to help individuals with medical problems. They admitted Clyde into their hospital and paid the hefty bill accrued through months of intensive treatments. Eventually his leg healed and Clyde was forever grateful. For the rest of his life Clyde never missed a chance to tell people about the kindness the Shriners demonstrated to him.

With testimonies like Clyde's it often proves difficult to convince people that Freemasonry is another form of divination. Keep in mind that Masonry is not a Christian organization because its teachings do not line up with the Word of God. "Masonry is not based on the Bible (referred to as "The Great Light"), but on the Kabala, the ultimate source of Masonic beliefs (Morals and Dogma), which is a medieval book of mysticism and magic. Masons require one to believe in God to be a member, but the candidate is never required to say what god he believes in. Masons commonly refer to their deity as the "Great Architect of the Universe" (G.A.O.T.U.) or the "Supreme Being." The name of Christ is seldom referred to in Masonic literature, apparently due to Masons not wanting to offend their non-Christian members. Freemasonry does not believe that Jesus Christ is God, nor that salvation is available only through Him.

"The reality of sin in the Biblical sense is denied. Masons think that any "shortcomings" can be overcome by greater enlightenment. Because they deny the reality of sin, Masons see no need for salvation in the Biblical sense. They see salvation as a step-by-step enlightenment, which comes through initiation into the Masonic degrees and their mysteries." [xli]

If Freemasonry runs in your background I encourage you to thoroughly renounce it. Some specific Masonic organizations include the women's Orders of the Eastern Star, the White Shrine of Jerusalem, the girls order of the Daughters of the Eastern Star, the International Orders of Job's Daughters, Rainbow Girls, and the boys Order of De Molay.

At a Freedom & Fullness Seminar a lady became angry and vehemently challenged the teaching that opposed Freemasonry. Then during the lunch break she decided to pray the prayer of renunciation found in the back of the syllabus just to see what would happen. As she prayed she suddenly got violently sick and threw up her lunch. Every time she attempted to resume the prayer she got ill all over again. Needless to say, it became apparent to her that something was dreadfully wrong. After the lunch break she anxiously awaited ministry and was in total agreement that Freemasonry had to go. (See Appendix for the prayer of renunciation.)

# Prayer

(Note: I encourage you to pray this prayer out loud in the presence of one or two Spirit-filled Christians who walk in the authority of Christ.)

*Heavenly Father, please forgive me for my involvement in divination. I turn away from all forms of divination. My sin was wicked, ungodly, and against You. But now I receive Your forgiveness. The blood of Jesus cleanses me now of the sin of divination and I am free and forgiven according to 1 John 1:9. Now I reject and renounce and break any agreement I or my ancestor made with the spirit of divination and all its underlings. (Name off all the forms of divination you circled in the above lists.) I command all divination to leave me now and go to dry places, in Jesus' name, Amen.*

# 29

---

# Many Forms of Fear

*When a strong man, fully armed, guards his own palace,*
*his goods are in peace. But when a stronger than he comes*
*upon him and overcomes him, he takes from him all his*
*armor in which he trusted, and divides his spoils.*

(Luke 11:21-22)

Recently I decided to dig up a small tree in my backyard because it was in the wrong location. As I dug around it I noticed a main taproot, so I cut through it with a pick ax. Then I tried to pull up the tree with a leverage system I rigged up. To my dismay the tree wouldn't budge. There were a lot of smaller roots about the size of my finger that held the tree tenaciously in place. Out of these smaller roots grew little hair like roots all of which worked together to keep me from pulling up the tree. After a lot more digging and chopping (and sweating) the tree was dislodged and came up out of the ground. Think of the stronghold of fear as a tree with a root system. The main root spirit of fear has other little roots branching off, underlings that hold it in place.

Just as a tap root has numerous smaller roots, so there are many forms of fear. Medical science has catalogued thousands of them. As a side note, the most common form of fear in our society is what we call stress. Remember that stress is a form of fear. We have already looked at other numerous forms of fear but there are many more.

If fear has established itself in your life it doesn't want to relinquish its hold on you so it sets up armor to keep it in place. The way it works is that a person may have the strongman of fear present in their life due to their own sin or the sins of their ancestors. The strongman gathers underlings that are under its authority. My uncle, Robert Peterson, had a deliverance ministry for many years and referred to the strongmen as "master controllers."

Don't get hung up on the terminology. The main truth is that there are root spirits that have a sphere of influence such as fear, infirmity, haughtiness, jealousy, etc., and they have lesser entities in place under their authority. These underlings help serve as their armor, so just going after the root spirit without addressing the underlings is often a work in futility.

Carefully consider the words of Jesus: *"When a strong man, fully armed, guards his own palace, his goods are in peace. But when a stronger than he comes upon him and overcomes him, he takes from him all his armor in which he trusted, and divides his spoils"* (Luke 11:21-22). The palace is the human being. The *stronger than he* is the believer, filled with the Spirit of God, walking in the authority of God. Notice that the first thing the Spirit-filled Christian does to expel the strongman is to take away his armor because the armor helps keep him in place.

That's why it presents itself as a major battle to cast out the strongman of fear without first dealing with the underlings. It has been my experience that when people address the specific underlings that are visibly at work in their lives, the strongman leaves without as much resistance. By dealing with the underlings it also helps the person maintain their deliverance.

Look at the following list of fears I often deal with when ministering to others.

## The Fear of:

| | |
|---|---|
| Abandonment | Suffocation |
| Rejection | Spiders |
| Poverty | Judgment |
| Anxiety | Condemnation |
| Thunder | Betrayal |
| Success | People's words |
| Inadequacy | Not getting delivered |
| Failure | Doctors |
| Insanity | Hospitals |
| Authority | Criticism |
| Men/women | Snakes |
| Loss of relationships | Heights |
| Being controlled | Strangling |
| Demons | Mice |
| Being manipulated | Losing friends |
| Dying process | Losing salvation |
| Mother | Disease |
| Natural disasters | Certain foods |
| False tongues | Choking to death |
| Father | Blood |
| Traffic Accident | Loss of a child |
| Vulnerability | Loss of spouse |
| Dentists | Not having enough |
| Facial expressions | Blindness |
| What people think | Ghosts |
| Bees | Public speaking |
| Homelessness | Wasted years |
| Losing job | Sex |
| Flying | Loss of being in control |
| Drowning | War |

Water

The unknown

Getting old

Floods

The dark

Losing face

Change

Lightning

Being shamed

Illness

Confrontation

Suicide

Trucks

The future

Vomiting

Punishment

Disfigurement

Death

Lack

Abandoning loved ones

Disability

through death or disease

## Related Traits:

Perfectionism

Worry

Timidity

Inadequacy

Shyness

Drivenness

Tension/stress

Nightmares

Easily frightened

Torment

Fear-faith

Performance orientation

Anxiety

We have already dealt with a number of these fears, but as you can see, there are many more to consider. Go over the list and circle the ones that pertain to you. If any other fears come to mind write them down. Then one at a time pray this prayer.

# Prayer

*Heavenly Father, I confess that coming into agreement with the fear of _____ was sin. I receive Your forgiveness and the blood of Jesus cleanses me now. I ask you to bring this fleshly tendency to death at the cross of Christ. Listen to me fear of _____, I address you in Jesus' name. Leave me now and go to dry places. I reject you, I renounce you, and I break any agreement I have made with you so go, in the name of Jesus. I place the cross of Christ between me and the iniquity of fear that was passed onto me through my generations past. Father in heaven, please show me Your truth about this specific fear, in Jesus' name, Amen.*

# 30

---

# Get to the Root

*Looking carefully lest anyone fall short of the grace of God; lest any root of bitterness springing up cause trouble, and by this many become defiled.*

(Hebrews 12:15)

So far we have been dealing primarily with mere underlings or associates of the root spirit of fear. In the natural if you don't destroy the main root, the tree is likely to grow back. I had a lovely pear tree growing in my front yard. I liked the tree but it was interfering with the growth of another tree I wanted to save. I hired an arborist to cut the pear tree down so that the remaining trunk was flush with the lawn. Shortly after the work was done, the roots sent up some suckers attempting to reestablish the tree. The lawn was mowed weekly which cut off the tender shoots. But week after week the shoots reappeared and this process went on for four or five years. Finally I did what was necessary to kill the root and the shoots have not returned.

If you want to get rid of a tree you don't simply pick the fruit. You don't even want to cut the branches off because pruning the tree only makes it healthier the next growing season. The tree will also survive if you cut out some of the subsidiary roots. You have to kill the main root.

Similarly, when attempting to conquer fear many people rely on merely defeating the associates of fear. They go after the troublesome manifestations or the symptoms of a deeper root problem.

The kingdom of darkness works off a root/fruit system: *Looking carefully lest anyone fall short of the grace of God; lest any **root** of bitterness springing up cause trouble, and by this many become defiled* (Hebrews 12:15). Where there is fruit look for a root. If fear keeps coming back make sure you have dealt with the root spirit.

The Kingdom of God also has a root/fruit structure: *But the fruit of the Spirit is love, joy, peace, longsuffering, kindness, goodness, faithfulness, gentleness, self-control...* (Galatians 5:22-23a). When we merely focus on producing good fruit we set ourselves up for frustration. If we would only yield ourselves to the Holy Spirit's control and be firmly rooted in Him, good fruit is a natural byproduct.

A branch doesn't strive to bear good fruit. It simply abides in the tree trunk and the trunk draws it nourishment from the roots and the fruit appears naturally. Satan counterfeits God's methods. So it follows that the opposite of the Holy Spirit is the fruit of the unholy spirit. Don't fall for his deception by focusing on destroying the fruit.

Once you have renounced the particular forms of fear you have identified in your life the next step is to go after the main root. I recommend the assistance of a Spirit-filled believer who understands spiritual authority.

## Prayer

Here is a suggested prayer for the one being prayed for. Make sure you pray out loud because evil spirits can't read your mind and they need to hear what you're saying:

*Spirit of fear, I reject you, I renounce you, and I break any agreement I or my ancestors made with you. I command you to leave me now and go to dry places, in Jesus' name, Amen.*

The prayer minister may say something like this:

*Spirit of fear, I bind you and your underlings together as one and I command you to go and not return. I lay the ax of the Holy Spirit to your root. (Use a prophetic hand motion to simulate an ax cutting the root in the stomach area.) I cut you off and pull you up by the roots; I break your power over this person's life; and I command you to go to dry places, in the name of Jesus. You will not linger in this room or go into any other person or animal but you must go out of this city. I command you to bow the knee to Jesus and come out. Go out with a breath, in Jesus' name!* [xlii]

Keep praying in this manner until you both sense a peace or release. After evicting the root spirit of fear the prayer minister should pray a prayer of blessing, releasing peace, love, courage, sound mind, power, and trust, asking God to seal what He has done.

# 31

---

# The Fear of the Lord

*Therefore, since we are receiving a kingdom which cannot be shaken, let us have grace, by which we may serve God acceptably with reverence and godly fear. For our God is a consuming fire.*

(Hebrews 12:28-29)

A good kind of fear presents itself in the Bible. Many blessings come when we fear the Lord. The fear of the Lord is not a cringing, cowering fear that makes us want to run away from God. Rather it is a healthy respect for what He says and an awe of who He is.

When I lived in the San Francisco Bay Area in California my son came home from Texas to visit. He brought some native Texan friends with him. Texans are "flat-landers" and these young people had never seen a real mountain. When they saw the hills in our town they commented on what it must be like to live in the mountains.

I chuckled, "Mountains! You think these are mountains? I need to show you some real mountains." So the next day we drove to Yosemite National Park in the High Sierras, about a four-hour drive.

Upon arriving in the Yosemite Valley we headed right to Half Dome. When we got out of the car and walked up the path for a better view what the kids saw took their breath away. We all stood there in awe beholding the magnitude of this famous mountain. Its beauty and greatness captured our attention entirely and we could only stare and drink in the experience. I have the same feeling when I visit such places as the Grand Canyon.

These kinds of experiences represent a little taste of what it is to behold the beauty and majesty of the Lord. When we get a glimpse of who God is, the only thing we can do is stand in awe of Him. That is the fear of the Lord: *Let all the earth fear the LORD; let all the inhabitants of the world stand in awe of Him* (Psalm 33:8).

The writer of Proverbs adds another dynamic to understanding the fear of the Lord: *The fear of the Lord is to hate evil* (Proverbs 8:13a). To fear the Lord means that we hate the things that God hates because we see their destructive nature. Another way to put it is we see the evil in the evil and we do all to avoid it. To hate evil is to turn away from it. *"And to man He said, 'Behold, the fear of the Lord, that is wisdom, and to depart from evil is understanding'"* (Job 28:28). *And by the fear of the LORD men depart from evil* (Proverbs 16:6b).

Blessings follow those who fear the Lord. Take a look at some of the benefits we receive from God when we fear Him.

1.  God delivers us from our enemies. *But the LORD your God you shall fear; and He will deliver you from the hand of all*

*your enemies* (2 Kings 17:39).

2. God sustains us in the time of trial. *Behold, the eye of the LORD is on those who fear Him, on those who hope in His mercy, to deliver their soul from death, and to keep them alive in famine* (Psalm 33:18-19).

3. God reveals intimate truths. *The secret of the LORD is with those who fear Him, and he will show them His covenant* (Psalm 25:14).

4. God provides our needs. *Oh, fear the LORD, you His saints! There is no want (lack) to those who fear Him. The young lions lack and suffer hunger; but those who seek the LORD shall not lack any good thing* (Psalm 34:9-10).

5. God pours out His mercy. *But the mercy of the LORD is from everlasting to everlasting on those who fear Him* (Psalm 103:17a).

6. God blesses our finances and our heritage. *Praise the LORD! Blessed is the man who fears the LORD, who delights greatly in His commandments. His descendants will be mighty on earth; the generation of the upright will be blessed. Wealth and riches will be in his house, and his righteousness endures forever* (Psalm 112:1-3). *By humility and the fear of the LORD are riches, and honor, and life* (Proverbs 22:4).

7. God prolongs our life. *The fear of the LORD prolongs days, but the years of the wicked will be shortened* (Proverbs 10:27).

8. God gives us confidence and security. *In the fear of the LORD there is strong confidence, and His children shall have a place of refuge* (Proverbs 14:26).

9. God keeps us from being touched by evil. *The fear of the LORD leads to life: Then one rests content, untouched by evil* (Proverbs 19:6, NIV).

## Prayer

*Father, please teach me the fear of the Lord. I want to have a healthy fear of You. Please forgive me for not giving You and Your Word rightful respect. Forgive me for not seeking to learn to fear You and stand in awe of You. I trust that You will show me experientially the fear of the Lord, in Jesus' name, Amen.*

# 32

---

# Closing Remarks

Congratulations on completing this book on conquering fear. I trust that you have already gained some significant victory. The results of these suggested exercises may or may not be immediately seen so let me encourage you to persevere.

If you have been walking in fear for most of your life, your mind has become programmed to respond to your environment in an unhealthy manner. This underscores the importance of renewing your mind on a daily basis. You have the authority, in Jesus, to reject thoughts of fear when they come to mind.

The more you learn to recognize when fearful thoughts bombard you, the easier it is to cast down those imaginations and bring your thoughts in submission to Jesus Christ. Be proactive and fight the good fight of faith. If you fail, don't go into condemnation. Don't be so hard on yourself. Eventually you will experience ever-increasing levels of freedom.

Though you need to recognize fearful thoughts when the enemy sends them your way, do not become sin conscious. In your attempt to gain victory your thoughts may become consumed with discovering fear. You may be doing some major spiritual surgery and, if so, it is natural to dwell on the various aspects of fear—but only for a season. It is imperative that you learn to focus most of your attention on God and His Kingdom principles.

Let me also encourage you to read my book, *Soul Pain: Exposing the Valueless Lie.* Valuelessness and fear go hand-in-hand, for Jesus said, *"But the very hairs of your head are all numbered. Fear ye not therefore, ye are of more value than many sparrows"* (Matthew 10:30-31, KJV). When you know in your heart how much value God has placed in you, your fears will dissipate.

Another important word of advice is that living free from fear won't make God love you any more than He does right now. Conversely, if you don't get complete victory over this damaging emotion, God will not love you any less. If you have received Jesus Christ as your Lord and Savior and if you have accepted His substitutionary death on the cross for your sins, then God has totally accepted you just the way you are. God wants you free, not so that He will accept you, but so that you will be able to walk in the joy and peace that He has for His people.

If you have never received Jesus in your heart and you would like to, say a simple prayer such as this: *God I acknowledge that I have sinned and that I need a savior. I choose to believe that Jesus died on the cross for my sins and that He rose again on the third day according to the Scriptures. I want Jesus to come into my heart and wash away all of my sins. I receive Him now and I want Him to be the Lord of my life. I give my heart to Jesus now and I thank You, Heavenly Father, for forgiving all my sins, past, present, and future, Amen.*

Once you've said this prayer, I encourage you to read your Bible daily, and to get into fellowship with other Christians who can help you in your daily walk. Welcome to the Kingdom!

# Appendix

**PRAYER OF RELEASE FOR FREEMASONS
AND THEIR DESCENDANTS**

*If you were once a Mason or are a descendant of a Mason, we recommend that you pray through the following prayer from your heart. Don't be like the Masons who are given their obligations and oaths one line at a time and without prior knowledge of the requirements. Please read it through first so you know what is involved. It is best to pray this aloud with a Christian witness or counselor present. We suggest a brief pause following each paragraph to allow the Holy Spirit to show any additional issues which may require attention.*

"Father God, creator of heaven and earth, I come to You in the name of Jesus Christ your Son. I come as a sinner seeking forgiveness and cleansing from all sins committed against You, and others made in Your image. I honor my earthly father and mother and all of my ancestors of flesh and blood, and of the spirit by adoption and godparents, but I utterly turn away from and renounce all their sins. I forgive all my ancestors for the effects of their sins on me and my children. I confess and renounce all of my own sins. I renounce Satan and every spiritual power of his affecting me and my family.

I renounce and forsake all involvements in Freemasonry or any other lodge or craft by my ancestors and myself. I renounce witchcraft, the principal spirit behind Freemasonry, and I renounce Baphomet, the Spirit of Antichrist and the curse of the Luciferian doctrine. I renounce the idolatry, blasphemy, secrecy and deception of Masonry at every level. I specifically renounce the insecurity, the love of position and power, the love of money, avarice or greed, and the pride which would have led my ancestors into Masonry, especially the fears of death, fears of men, and fears of trusting, in the name of Jesus Christ.

I renounce every position held in the lodge by any of my ancestors, including "Tyler," "Master," "Worshipful Master," or any other. I renounce the calling of any man "Master," for Jesus Christ is my only master and Lord, and He forbids anyone else having that title. I renounce the entrapping of others into Masonry, and observing the helplessness of others during the rituals. I renounce the effects of Masonry passed on to me through any female ancestor who felt distrusted and rejected by her husband as he entered and attended any lodge and refused to tell her of his secret activities.

## 1st Degree

I renounce the oaths taken and the curses involved in the First or Entered Apprentice degree, especially their effects on the throat and tongue. I renounce the Hoodwink, the blindfold, and its effects on emotions and eyes, including all confusion, fear of the dark, fear of the light, and fear of sudden noises. I renounce the secret word BOAZ, and all it means. I renounce the mixing and mingling of truth and error, and the blasphemy of this degree of Masonry. I renounce the noose around the neck, the fear of choking and also every spirit causing asthma, hay fever, emphysema or any other breathing difficulty. I renounce the compass point, sword or spear held against the breast, the fear of death by stabbing pain, and the fear of heart attack from this degree. In the name of Jesus Christ I now pray for healing of... (throat, vocal cords, nasal passages, sinus, bronchial tubes, etc.) for healing of the speech area, and the release of the Word of God to me and through me and my family.

## 2nd Degree

I renounce the oaths taken and the curses involved in the second or Fellow Craft degree of Masonry, especially the curses on the heart and chest. I renounce the secret words JACHIN and SHIBBOLETH and all that these mean. I cut off emotional hardness, apathy, indifference, unbelief, and deep anger from me and my family. In the name of Jesus Christ I pray for the healing of... (the chest/lung/heart area) and also for the healing of my emotions, and ask to be made sensitive to the Holy Spirit of God.

## 3rd Degree

I renounce the oaths taken and the curses involved in the third or Master Mason degree, especially the curses on the stomach and womb area. I renounce the secret words MAHA BONE, MACHABEN, MACHBINNA and TUBAL CAIN, and all that they mean. I renounce the spirit of death from the blows to the head enacted as ritual murder, the fear of death, false martyrdom, fear of violent gang attack, assault, or rape, and the helplessness of this degree. I renounce the falling into the coffin or stretcher involved in the ritual murder. I renounce the false resurrection of this degree, because only Jesus Christ is the Resurrection and the Life! I also renounce the blasphemous kissing of the Bible on a Witchcraft oath. I cut off all spirits of death, witchcraft and deception and in the name of Jesus Christ I pray for the healing of...(the stomach, gall bladder, womb, liver, and any other organs of my body affected by Masonry), and I ask for a release of compassion and understanding for me and my family.

## Holy Royal Arch Degree

I renounce and forsake the oaths taken and the curses involved in the Holy Royal Arch Degree of Masonry, especially the oath regarding the removal of the head from the body and the exposing of the brains to the hot sun. I renounce the Mark Lodge, and the mark in the form of squares and angles, which marks the person for life. I also reject the jewel or talisman which may have been made from this mark sign and worn at lodge meetings. I renounce the false secret name of God, JAHBULON, and the password, AMMI RUHAMAH and all they mean. I renounce the false communion or Eucharist taken in this degree, and all the mockery, skepticism and unbelief about the redemptive work of Jesus Christ on the cross of Calvary. I cut off all these curses and their effects on me and my family in the name of Jesus Christ, and I pray for…(healing of the brain, the mind, etc.)

## 18th Degree

I renounce the oaths taken and the curses involved in the eighteenth degree of Masonry, the Most Wise Sovereign Knight of the Pelican and the Eagle and Sovereign Prince Rose Croix of Heredom. I renounce and reject the Pelican witchcraft spirit, as well as the occultic influence of the Rosicrucians and the Kabbala in this degree. I renounce the claim that the death of Jesus Christ was a "dire calamity," and also the deliberate mockery and twisting of the Christian doctrine of the Atonement. I renounce the blasphemy and rejection of the deity of Jesus Christ, and the secret words IGNE NATURA RENOVATUR and its burning. I renounce the mockery of the communion taken in this degree, including a biscuit, salt and white wine.

## 30th Degree

I renounce the oaths taken and the curses involved in the thirtieth degree of Masonry, the Grand Knight Kadosh and Knight of the Black and White Eagle. I renounce the password, "STIBIUM ALKABAR ," and all it means.

## 31st Degree

I renounce the oaths taken and the curses involved in the thirty-first degree of Masonry, the Grand Inspector Inquisitor

Commander. I renounce all the gods and goddesses of Egypt which are honored in this degree, including Anubis with the ram's head, Osiris the Sun god, Isis the sister and wife of Osiris and also the moon goddess. I renounce the Soul of Cheres, the false symbol of immortality, the Chamber of the dead and the false teaching of reincarnation.

## 32nd Degree

I renounce the oaths taken and the curses involved in the thirty-second degree of Masonry, the Sublime Prince of the Royal Secret. I renounce Masonry's false Trinitarian deity AUM, and its parts; Brahma the creator, Vishnu the preserver and Shiva the destroyer. I renounce the deity of AHURA-MAZDA, the claimed spirit or source of all light, and the worship with fire, which is an abomination to God, and also the drinking from a human skull in many Rites.

## York Rite

I renounce the oaths taken and the curses involved in the York Rite of Freemasonry, including Mark Master, Past Master, Most Excellent Master, Royal Master, Select Master, Super Excellent Master, the Orders of the Red Cross, the Knights of Malta, and the Knights Templar degrees. I renounce the vows taken on a human skull, the crossed swords, and the curse and death wish of Judas of having the head cut off and placed on top of a church spire. I renounce the unholy communion and especially of drinking from a human skull in many Rites.

## Shriners (America only—doesn't apply in other countries)

I renounce the oaths taken and the curses and penalties involved in the Ancient Arabic Order of the Nobles of the Mystic Shrine. I renounce the piercing of the eyeballs with a three-edged blade, the flaying of the feet, the madness, and the worship of the false god Allah as the god of our fathers. I renounce the hoodwink, the mock hanging, the mock beheading, the mock drinking of the blood of the victim, the mock dog urinating on the initiate, and the offering of urine as a commemoration.

## 33rd Degree

I renounce the oaths taken and the curses involved in the thirty-third degree of Masonry, the Grand Sovereign Inspector General. I renounce and forsake the declaration that Lucifer is God. I renounce the cable-tow around the neck. I renounce the death wish that the wine drunk from a human skull should turn to poison and the skeleton whose cold arms are invited if the oath of this degree is violated. I renounce the three infamous assassins of their grandmaster, law, property and religion, and the greed and witchcraft involved in the attempt to manipulate and control the rest of mankind.

## All other degrees

I renounce all the other oaths taken, the rituals of every other degree and the curses involved. I renounce all other lodges and secret societies such as Prince Hall Freemasonry, Mormonism, The Order of Amaranth, Oddfellows, Buffalos, Druids, Foresters, Orange, Elks, Moose and Eagles Lodges, the Ku Klux Klan, The Grange, The Woodmen of the World, Riders of the Red Robe, The Knights of Pythias, The Mystic Order of the Veiled Prophets of the Enchanted Realm, the women's Orders of the Eastern Star, and of the White Shrine of Jerusalem, the girls' Order of the Daughters of the Eastern Star, the International Orders of Job's Daughters, and of the Rainbow, and the boys' Order of De Molay, and their effects on me and all my family.

I renounce the ancient pagan teaching and symbolism of the First Tracing Board, the Second Tracing Board and the Third Tracing Board used in the ritual of the Blue Lodge. I renounce the pagan ritual of the "Point with a Circle" with all its bondages and phallus worship. I renounce the occultic mysticism of the black and white mosaic chequered floor with the tessellated boarder and five-pointed blazing star. I renounce the symbol "G" and its veiled pagan symbolism and bondages. I renounce and utterly forsake the Great Architect of the Universe, who is revealed in the higher degrees as Lucifer, and his false claim to be the universal fatherhood of God. I also renounce the false claim that Lucifer is the Morning Star and Shining One and I declare that Jesus Christ is the Bright and Morning Star of Revelation 22:16.

I renounce the All-Seeing Third Eye of Freemasonry of Horus in the forehead and its pagan and occult symbolism. I renounce all false communions taken, all mockery of the redemptive work of Jesus Christ on the cross of Calvary, all unbelief, confusion and depression, and all worship of Lucifer as God. I renounce and forsake the lie of Freemasonry that man is not sinful, but merely imperfect, and so can redeem himself through good works. I rejoice that the Bible states that I cannot do a single thing to earn my salvation, but that I can only be saved by grace through faith in Jesus Christ and what He accomplished on the Cross of Calvary.

I renounce all fear of insanity, anguish, death wishes, suicide and death in the name of Jesus Christ. Death was conquered by Jesus Christ, and He alone holds the keys of death and hell, and I rejoice that He holds my life in His hands now. He came to give me life abundantly and eternally, and I believe His promises.

I renounce all anger, hatred, murderous thoughts, revenge, retaliation, spiritual apathy, false religion, all unbelief, especially unbelief in the Holy Bible as God's Word, and all compromise of God's Word. I renounce all spiritual searching into false religions, and all striving to please God. I rest in the knowledge that I have found my Lord and Savior Jesus Christ, and that He has found me.

I will burn all objects in my possession which connect me with all lodges and occultic organizations, including Masonry, Witchcraft and Mormonism, and all regalia, aprons, books of rituals, rings and other jewelry. I renounce the effects these or other objects of Masonry, such as the compass, the square, the noose, or the blindfold have had on me or my family in Jesus' Name.

*All participants should now be invited to sincerely carry out the following:*

(1) Symbolically remove the blindfold (hoodwink) and give it to the Lord for disposal;

(2) In the same way, symbolically remove the veil of mourning;

(3) Symbolically cut and remove the noose from around the neck, gather it up with the cable-tow running down the body and give it all to the Lord for His disposal;

(4) Renounce the false Freemasonry marriage covenant, removing from the 4th finger of the right hand the ring of this false marriage covenant, giving it to the Lord to dispose of it;

(5) Symbolically remove the chains and bondages of Freemasonry from the body;

(6) Symbolically remove all Freemasonry regalia and armor, especially the Apron;

(7) Invite participants to repent of and seek forgiveness for having walked on all unholy ground, including Freemasonry lodges and temples, including any Mormon or other occultic/Masonic organizations.

(8) Symbolically remove the ball and chain from the ankles.

(9) Proclaim that Satan and his demons no longer have any legal rights to mislead and manipulate the person/s seeking help.

Holy Spirit, I ask that you show me anything else which I need to do or to pray so that I and my family may be totally free from the consequences of the sins of Masonry, Witchcraft, Mormonism and Paganism.

*(Pause while listening to God, and pray as the Holy Spirit leads you.)*

Now dear Father God, I ask humbly for the blood of Jesus Christ, Your Son, to cleanse me from all these sins I have confessed and renounced, to cleanse my spirit, my soul, my mind, my emotions, and every part of my body which has been affected by these sins, in Jesus' name!

I renounce every evil spirit associated with Masonry and Witchcraft and all other sins, and I command in the name of Jesus Christ for Satan and every evil spirit to be bound and to leave me now, touch or harming no one, and go to the place appointed for you by the Lord Jesus, never to return to me or my family. I call on the name of the Lord Jesus to be delivered of these spirits, in accordance with the many promises of the Bible. I ask to be delivered of every spirit of sickness, infirmity, curse, affliction, addiction, disease or allergy associated with these sins I have confessed and renounced. I surrender to God's Holy Spirit and to no other spirit all the places in my life where these sins have been. I ask you, Lord, to baptize me in Your Holy Spirit now according to the promises in your Word. I take to myself the whole armor of God in accordance with Ephesians Chapter Six, and rejoice in its protections as Jesus surrounds me and fills me with His Holy Spirit. I enthrone You, Lord Jesus, in my heart, for You are my Lord and my Savior, the source of eternal life. Thank You, Father God, for Your mercy, Your forgiveness, and Your love, in the name of Jesus Christ. Amen.

*(This prayer is taken from "Unmasking Freemasonry—Removing the Hoodwink," by Selwyn Stevens, (ISBN 0 83417-3-7) published by Jubilee Publishers, P.O. Box 36-044, Wellington 6330, New Zealand. Copying of this prayer is both permitted and encouraged provided reference is made to where it comes from. Written testimonies of changed lives and healings are welcome.)*

# Notes

## Introduction

i.     Andrew Wommack, *A Better Way to Pray,* tape series, tape #Y24, "Speak To The Mountain," Andrew Wommack Ministries, 2003.

## CHAPTER ONE

ii.     The *New International Version,* (Grand Rapids, MI: Zondervan, 1973, 1978, 1984 by International Bible Society).

## CHAPTER TWO

iii.     Iniquity is different than sin. Iniquity refers to a propensity that is handed down to us from previous generations that may develop into destructive patterns of living. It refers to a twisted way of living or a bent toward evil in the life of the individual.

## CHAPTER FOUR

iv.     Please note that, just as there exists a good kind of fear, there can also be anxiety, in the modern sense of the vernacular, that helps push us to the next level of growth. This form of anxiety is beneficial when it is temporary and nudges us along the path to greater maturity. An excellent book entitled, *Living From the Heart Jesus Gave You,* states it this way: "By knowing that anxiety is a normal passing between maturity stages allows a whole new energy that actually propels the maturity process." James G. Friesen, E. James Wilder, Anne M. Bierling, Rick

Koepcke, and Maribeth Poole, *Living From the Heart Jesus Gave You,* (Pasadena, CA: Shepherd's House, Revised 2000 R), p. 42.

v.    W.E. Vines, *Expository Dictionary of New Testament Words,* (Westwood, NJ: Fleming H. Revell Company, 1966), p. 168.

vi.    W.E. Vines, p. 288.

## CHAPTER FIVE

vii.    Croft M. Pentz, *The Complete Book of Zingers,* (Wheaton, IL: Tyndale House Publishers, 1990), p. 367.

## CHAPTER SIX

viii.    The *Amplified Bible,* (Grand Rapids, MI: Zondervan Publishing House, 1965).

## CHAPTER EIGHT

ix.    Henry Wright, *A More Excellent Way,* (Thomaston, GA: Pleasant Valley Publication, 2000), pp. 126, 144-145, 223.

## CHAPTER TEN

x.    The *New International Version.*

## CHAPTER ELEVEN

xi.    Elisabeth Kubler-Ross. From a lecture on "Death in a Death-Denying Society" given at Johns Hopkins University.

## CHAPTER TWELVE

xii.    Claire Weekes, *Pass Through Panic,* (Minneapolis, MN:

High Bridge Company) 2002, CD, original material: 1967. Dr. Weekes was a pioneer in panic disorders and has written related books, *Peace from Nervous Suffering and Hope and Help for Your Nerves.*

xiii.    Thomas A. Richards, The Anxiety Network International website, 2006.

xiv.    National Institute of Mental Health, 2005.

xv.    Thomas A. Richards, The Anxiety Network International website, 2006.

xvi.    National Institute of Mental Health, 1999.

xvii.    Claire Weekes, *Pass Through Panic.*

xviii.    Thomas A. Richards.

xix.    Olen Griffing.

xx.    Olen Griffing. Pastor Griffing has seen great success in dealing with people who suffer from panic attacks.

CHAPTER THIRTEEN

xxi.    Daniel C. Steere *Power for Living,* (Old Tappan, NJ: Fleming H. Revell Company, 1977), p. 116.

CHAPTER FOURTEEN

xxii.    Pacific Wrecks Forum, *pacificwrecks.com.*

CHAPTER FIFTEEN

xxiii.    James Barter, *The Golden Gate Bridge,* (San Diego, CA: Lucent Books, Inc., 2001), pp. 82-87.

xxiv.   Melvin Newland, *Sermon Central.com*

xxv.   The conditions are laid out within the context of the particular promise. For example, the promise in Philippians 4:19, "But my God shall supply all your need according to his riches in glory," is resting upon what he just said previously about their willingness to give offerings. In other words if we generously give to God's work we can expect Him to supply all our needs.

CHAPTER SIXTEEN

xxvi.   King Duncan, *Lively Illustrations for Effective Preaching,* (Knoxville, TN: Seven Worlds Publishing, 1987), p. 173.

xxvii.   Henry Wright, *Asteroids and the Bible,* (Thomaston, GA: Pleasant Valley Publications, 2002), pp. 7-10.

xxviii.   Wright, pp. 7-10.

CHAPTER TWENTY

xxix.   Henry Wright, *A More Excellent Way,* (Thomaston, GA: Pleasant Valley Publications, 2000), p. 142.

xxx.   Mark Virkler, Communion with God Ministries Newsletter, May/June 2011. "Insights from the Greek and Hebrew."

CHAPTER TWENTY-ONE

xxxi.   Vision Life Ministries, under the direction of Dr. Henry Malone, has developed a kit to help you cleanse your land.

CHAPTER TWENTY-THREE

xxxii.   University of Cambridge Counselling Service 1998, revised 2000 & 2005, website.

xxxiii. Adaptation from the University of Cambridge Counselling Service 1998, revised 2000 & 2005, website.

CHAPTER TWENTY-EIGHT

xxxiv. Henry Malone, *Shadow Boxing,* (Irving, TX: Vision Life Publications, 1999), pp. 126-127.

xxxv. John Ankerberg & John Weldon, *Encylopedia of New Age Beliefs,* (Eugene Publishers, 1996), p. 596.

xxxvi. Dave Fetcho, *Yoga,* (Berkeley, CA: Spiritual Counterfeits Project, 1978).

xxxvii. John Ankerberg & John Weldon, p. 593.

xxxviii. Hans Reiker, *The Yoga of Light: Hatha Yoga Pradipika,* (New York: Seabury Press, 1971).

xxxix. John Ankerberg & John Weldon, p. 17.

xl. Benjamin B. Wolman, Mantague Ullman, eds., *Handbook of States of Consciousness,* (New York: Van Nostrand Reinhold, 1986).

xli. Bill Keller, *Liveprayer Daily Devotional,* radio broadcast.

CHAPTER THIRTY

xlii. This is the prayer taught by Henry Malone in Personal Ministry Training seminars.

For additional copies of
**Conquering Fear**
contact
roger.frye@sbcglobal.net


For more information

**Roger Frye
1208 Clearwood Court
Allen, TX 75002
roger.frye@sbcglobal.net**

# Don't Forget!

*Get the most from this series by purchasing your copy of both the companion book to Conquering Fear,*

## "Soul Pain"

*As well as the*

## "Leadership Manual"

*for this life-changing series!*

CPSIA information can be obtained at www.ICGtesting.com
Printed in the USA
LVOW070201080212

267614LV00001B/3/P